Clifford K. Madsen's Contributions to Music Education and Music Therapy

Clifford K. Madsen's Contributions to Music Education and Music Therapy: Love of Learning summarizes the life and work of Dr. Clifford Madsen, a luminary in music education and author of a dozen books, the first recipient of the Senior Researcher Award from the Music Educators National Conference, and a mentor and teacher to generations of music educators and music therapists. This text presents Madsen's philosophy, career, and legacy through an exploration of primary sources and extensive interviews with former students, outlining the philosophical tenets Madsen espouses while contextualizing those tenets within his teachings, research, and service. What began as an exercise to record Madsen's work for archival purposes resulted in a study of how his philosophy manifested in a significant offering to music educators.

Throughout a prolific academic career, Dr. Madsen has led Florida State University to a position of preeminence in the fields of music education and music therapy. Yet as detailed here, his greatest impact goes beyond lesson plans and syllabi, epitomized by a love of learning. As Bob Duke stated, "What is monumental about Cliff is not what he has written. It is what he has done as a human being for other human beings."

Jessica Nápoles is Associate Professor of Choral Music Education and Conductor of the Concert Choir at the University of North Texas.

Rebecca B. MacLeod is Professor of Music Education at the University of North Carolina Greensboro.

Clifford K. Madsen's Contributions to Music Education and Music Therapy

Love of Learning

Jessica Nápoles and Rebecca B. MacLeod

Routledge
Taylor & Francis Group
NEW YORK AND LONDON

First published 2020
by Routledge
605 Third Avenue, New York, NY 10017

and by Routledge
2 Park Square, Milton Park, Abingdon, Oxon, OX14 4RN

First issued in paperback 2021

Routledge is an imprint of the Taylor & Francis Group, an informa business

Publisher's Note
The publisher has gone to great lengths to ensure the quality of this reprint but points out that some imperfections in the original copies may be apparent.

Library of Congress Cataloging-in-Publication Data
Names: Nápoles, Jessica, author. | MacLeod, Rebecca B., author.
Title: Clifford K. Madsen's contributions to music education and music therapy : love of learning / Jessica Nápoles and Rebecca B. MacLeod.
Description: New York : Routledge, 2020. | Includes bibliographical references and index.
Identifiers: LCCN 2019057278 (print) | LCCN 2019057279 (ebook) | ISBN 9780367857752 (hardback) | ISBN 9781003015024 (ebook)
Subjects: LCSH: Madsen, Clifford K. | Music teachers—United States—Biography. | Music therapists—United States—Biography. | Music—Instruction and study—Psychological aspects. | Music—Psychological aspects.
Classification: LCC ML423.M1075 N36 2020 (print) | LCC ML423.M1075 (ebook) | DDC 780.92—dc23
LC record available at https://lccn.loc.gov/2019057278
LC ebook record available at https://lccn.loc.gov/2019057279

ISBN 13: 978-1-03-223827-2 (pbk)
ISBN 13: 978-0-367-85775-2 (hbk)

Typeset in Times New Roman
by Apex CoVantage, LLC

Contents

Preface

In 2015, we decided we wanted video recordings of Dr. Clifford Madsen's Behavior Modification class across a full semester. We wanted to revisit the content associated with his *Teaching/Discipline* text, and also wanted a formal record of his teaching for archival purposes. While recording the class, we decided to expand the project and interview some of his former doctoral students, thinking we might publish an article about Clifford's legacy (this project ultimately became a version of Chapter 7). We realized that Clifford's story could not be limited to an article. We knew that a book would be a difficult endeavor, and that this project would take us many years. We also knew there was no way to include everyone who has been a student, colleague, or loved one, because Clifford Madsen has impacted so many people. Ultimately, we chose some who studied very closely with him across a substantial span of time. In some cases, we also included individuals with whom he had briefer but very impactful relationships. We know there is still much more to tell, and we know there are so many more people we could have interviewed, but time was a limitation. We are pleased to present this labor of love in its current form.

Acknowledgements

We are so grateful to the following people who have helped us make this project possible:

Mary Chandler: You are such a lovely person, and we loved reading all about your family history. Thank you for sharing "The Lives of My Parents" with us.

Seth Pendergast, Monica Valdes, and Julia Reeves: Thank you for hours and hours of interview transcriptions.

David Miller: Thank you for your assistance with the "Legacy" chapter, and your many hours sifting through interviews to help us make sense of the contents.

Chandler Bridges: Thank you for your videography expertise, and for the time spent recording Dr. Madsen's teaching.

Thank you to all of the wonderful people we interviewed for this project: former students, Al, Mary, Sitka, Cort, and Katia. We learned so much about Cliff, and could not be more excited to share your insights and stories.

And finally, to Cliff. You have inspired us for so many years. Thank you for sharing so generously with us your time, stories, pictures, wisdom, and love. We feel very fortunate to have studied with you, and to continue to learn and grow so much as a result of your tutelage. We are honored to have had the privilege to write this book to honor you and your legacy. We love you so much.

Introduction

Clifford Madsen is a well-known figure in the fields of music education and music therapy. The author of 12 books and over 200 articles, a leader in national organizations for music education and music therapy, the first recipient of the prestigious Senior Researcher Award granted by the Music Educators National Conference, and a mentor and teacher for generations of music educators, music therapists, teacher educators, and researchers, Clifford has truly influenced the fields of music education and music therapy. In his study documenting research productivity of music education researchers and the affiliations of authors' terminal degrees, Grashel (2007) writes that Florida State University (FSU) has been the most influential institution regarding publication in the *Journal of Research in Music Education* since 1990, and that Clifford has led FSU to its preeminent position in music education research through his, his colleagues', and his students' contributions to the research literature.

What is even more fascinating than his prolific academic career is how he became the man he is today. How did a young man from Price, Utah, who was unable to read until the third grade, who failed algebra three times and graduated eighth from the bottom of his graduating class, go on to become a prolific writer and a leading figure in quantitative research? How does one begin a career as a trumpet and horn performer, teach applied lessons at the university level, then transition into the field of music psychology and behavioral research? As we wrote this book, we completed hours of interviews, sifted through file after file, reread Dr. Madsen's various publications, found poems and letters from loved ones and students, reviewed his syllabi and grading practices, and observed his university classes. Through this process it became clear that love, genuine love, is at the epicenter of Clifford's teaching. He views the world through a combination of his philosophical views, personal values, and empirical evidence, which influenced how we chose to write this book. While his impact on these professions has been expansive, one of his dear friends, Robert Duke, aptly shared that

"What is monumental about Cliff is not what he has written. It is what he has done as a human being for other human beings" (Duke, Robert. Personal Interview. 7 May 2016). How does one measure the success of one's life, but through the impact that one has had on others? Clifford Madsen has made a tremendous and profound impact on those he has touched. We subtitled this book *Love of Learning*, because Clifford so clearly embodies being a lifelong learner himself. His students also pass on the many things they have learned from him, continuing his legacy. Alice-Ann Darrow wrote,

> When I think of who was most influential to my teaching in music education, it was without a doubt Clifford Madsen. I find myself often repeating things he said in class to my students, with attributions to him of course. He is an inspired and passionate teacher to be sure. I never wanted to miss anything he said in class. I know I sat in on two courses multiple semesters, just to be sure I didn't miss anything.
>
> (Darrow, Alice-Ann. Personal Interview. 29 October 2019)

Between the years 2015 and 2019, we interviewed Clifford Madsen, Mary Madsen, Katia Madsen, Cort Madsen, Sitka Madsen, 43 of his former doctoral students, and select acquaintances for the purpose of writing his biography. Clifford was intimately involved as a collaborator in this book, reviewing each chapter and contributing edits along the way. We hope that this biography illuminates the life and work of Clifford Madsen, who is deeply loved and respected by those around him.

Part I

Biographical Sketch

1 The Madsen Family

The story of young Clifford Madsen is one of a "late bloomer" who grew up in a large family that highly valued education. Born and reared in Price, Utah, his family were members of the Mormon Church. He was taught the values of kindness and generosity at a young age, and has continued to practice those principles throughout his life. He married his high school sweetheart, Mary Marakis, and they raised three children together—Sitka, Cort, and Katia. Clifford was born 3 May 1937 in the coal mining town of Price. Clifford's parents were Charles Henry Madsen, Sr. (1890–1982) and Lenora Roberts Kimball Madsen (1908–1986). He was one of 12 children.

Father: Charles Henry Madsen, Sr.

Charles H. Madsen, Sr. (Figure 1.1) was born in Ephraim, Utah, on 26 August 1890, and attended Snow Academy before entering teaching. He had two wives prior to Lenora. He married Mabel Ivie on 29 November 1911, and they had twin girls (Myrtle and Mabel). Mabel, his first wife, died the day after childbirth from kidney failure, and baby Mabel died shortly after. Zina Christensen was his second wife, whom he married on 14 February 1917. They had four daughters—Lora, Mildred ("Millie"), Josephine, and Charlene. Zina developed a toxic goiter when her five girls were still young. She died on 9 November 1930.

In 1932, Charles was the principal of Southside School, and Lenora Kimball was a teacher at the same school. During her time there, Lenora underwent an operation because she broke her ankle, and Charles offered to drive her from her apartment to school and back while she recovered. She told him how much the trips meant to her and thanked him for all of his help. Charles, 18 years her senior, had no idea she could be interested in him. He especially wondered if she would be willing to take on the work of raising his five daughters, and he knew that he needed help and a companion. They married on 2 June 1932, and had seven more children together: Charles Jr. ("Charley"), Mary, Clifford, Lenora ("Kaye"), Stanford, Carolyn, and Robert (see Figures 1.2 and 1.3).

Figure 1.1 Photo of Charles Henry Madsen, Sr.

Figure 1.2 Lenora and Charles Madsen

Charles held a variety of jobs and service commitments throughout his life. He was a principal in Price schools for 34 years, first including Southside Elementary (grades 1–6), Harding Elementary (grades 4–6), and Central Elementary (grades 1–3). Later, because of a growing population, the

DAD'S WIVES AND CHILDREN

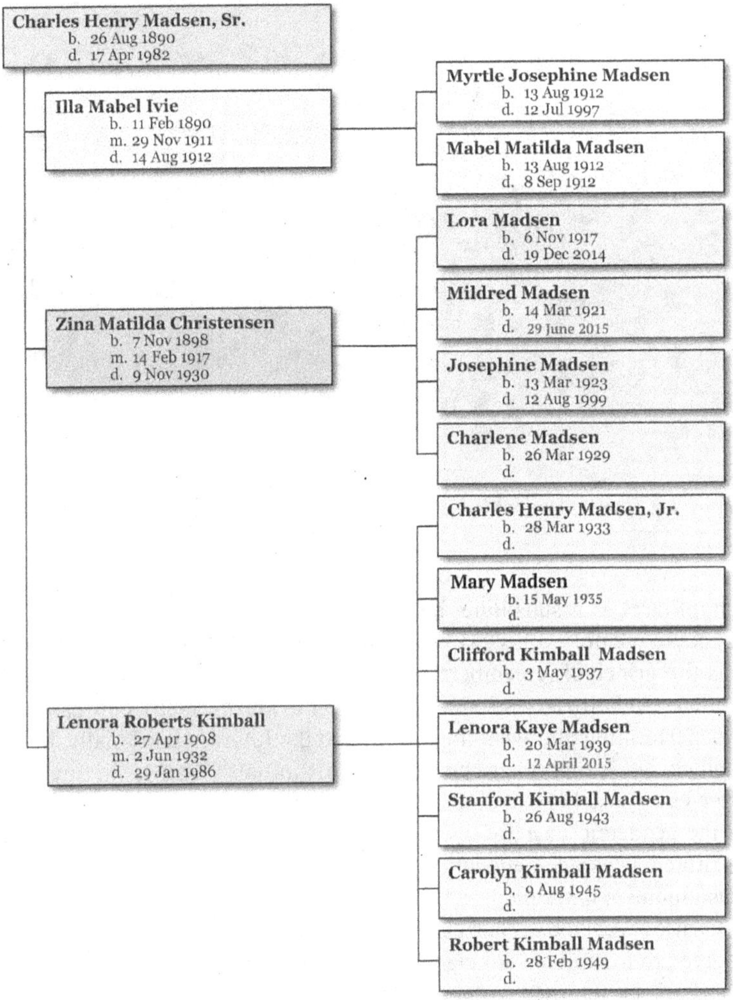

Figure 1.3 Genealogy[1]

Carbon County School Board appointed a Southside principal, thereby leaving Charles with just the Harding and Central schools that shared the same city block in downtown Price.

Charles Madsen was devoted to his students (Figure 1.4). When a teacher missed a day, Charles would substitute teach the class. During

Figure 1.4 Charles Henry Madsen, Sr. and students of Southside Elementary School

school days as a substitute, he recited poetry, having committed sundry poems to memory. Every student who went through any school where he was the principal remembers his rich baritone voice reciting poems. He graded standardized tests himself, in order to know exactly how each child was performing and what they needed in the future. Additionally, he read each student's report card and marked his initials, "CHM," in tiny letters after every teacher's entry. He went through this procedure every term of the academic year for every student during his entire tenure. He also instituted a character education program in the elementary schools, which was unique at that time.

Charles received a Bachelor of Science in Educational Administration degree from Brigham Young University (BYU). Even after he retired as principal, he returned to the classroom to teach English at Cyprus High School, and received an outstanding teacher award at age 72. When asked about his philosophy, he stated:

> I had somewhat the same idea as Joseph Smith had about the LDS church, when asked how he controlled so many people. He said he taught them correct principles and they governed themselves. I taught my teachers to place children in the center of the stage, not subject

> matter. We organized a child-centered curriculum in which the children were the focal point of the entire program.[2]

A faithful member of the Rotary Club, Charles began as an education leader, then went on to become Secretary, then President. In this position, he proposed that the community build a swimming pool for children because they were swimming in a filthy public canal. The Rotary Club members met weekly to discuss issues facing the community. At these meetings, there was always a musical moment. Members of the club rotated responsibility for facilitating these programs, and Charles would call on his son Clifford when it was his "night at the Rotary." Clifford became well known among the Rotarians as a fine trumpet player and orator.

Charles was also committed to removing prostitution from the city of Price, and he did. As a mayoral candidate, Charles, as had many before him, ran on the platform of cleaning out the prostitutes. Others had said the same thing—although it was tacitly assumed they would never do it. Not Charles Madsen: When he won the election, he did just that. He gave every known prostitute a one-way ticket out of town. He served one term in 1926–1927. During this time, he carried a gun for self-protection; such was the condition of Carbon County. It was perhaps the only place in the state of Utah where open gambling and prostitution coexisted with a group of other folks that included the Madsens.

During the school's summer recess, Charles Madsen sold encyclopedias to help support the family. He also worked as a soil engineer at the Scofield Dam. After retirement from education, he went back to soil testing when the family moved to Bountiful, Utah. He was always exceedingly competent and quickly became the best person at this task. He even trained some of the new engineers who were studying at the University of Utah.

As for his religious beliefs, Charles and his family were strong believers of the Mormon/Latter-day Saints (LDS) teachings. He believed that:

> Our family was taught by example and precept that we are our brothers' keepers, and the solidarity of the group has stood the test of years. The older children helped the younger ones to reach goals that would never have been possible without this assistance.[3]

Charles Madsen involved his sons in the Boy Scouts of America, and both of his sons rose to the rank of Eagle Scout. In fact, Clifford Madsen was the youngest scouting member in Utah to achieve that rank (see Figure 1.5), something of which he and his father were quite proud.

Scouting is a Family Affair

Typical of the father-sons interest in the Boy Scout movement in the Carbon district, a movement which will be encouraged to interest more fathers as leaders and more sons as Boy Scouts in the next few weeks as the Boy Scout fund drive gets underway, is Charles Madsen, Sr., and his two sons, Charles, Jr., left, and Clifford K. Mr. Madsen is commissioner of Boy Scouts in the Carbon district of the Utah National Parks council and his two sons are both Eagles with Charles, Jr., having earned two palm leaves and Clifford believed to be the youngest boy in this district ever to climb into the Eagle's nest.

Figure 1.5 Scouting: Charley, Charles, and Clifford

Mother: Lenora Roberts Kimball Madsen

Clifford's mother Lenora (Figure 1.6) was born in St. David, Arizona, and was reared in a family of ten children. Her parents were farmers. Intellectually advanced, she skipped a grade and completed a four-year high school program in three years. Lenora was a teacher in the Elsinore, Rains, Columbia, and Wellington school districts in Utah before moving to Price. She is quoted as saying "Teaching, to me, is a privilege, rather than a means to an end. No other field offers such a fertile place to build character as does teaching."[4] It is said that every student wanted to be in her fifth-grade class (see Figure 1.7). When other teachers struggled with "problem students," those students were placed in Lenora's class. She was extremely creative; during World War II, she put together a variety show consisting of fifth graders that toured the state. This endeavor raised $10,000 for war bonds.

In addition to her commitment to teaching, Lenora loved to write poems and stories. She wrote many poems, and *Green-Eye Phantoms* was one of her most popular books. The local newspaper recognized it as a great book for children.

Figure 1.6 Lenora Madsen

Figure 1.7 Lenora (top right) with her students

Lenora's generosity has been mentioned repeatedly by her children and family members. Many of her children relay the times they remember taking clothing and other items to needy families in the community, and how there were always a number of people over for Thanksgiving who would otherwise be spending the holiday alone. She also demanded that the children say something positive before launching into criticism. Lenora taught her children not just to get along, but to truly love each other. She taught them to be inclusive and to treat people with respect. During one of Clifford's classes, he said that he was very lucky as a child to have had a delightfully romantic and somewhat zany mother and an extremely proper father. Clifford remembers that during a time of financial difficulty, his mother had two dresses, and she would wash one every night so that she would have one to wear the next day. Lenora rarely spent money on herself. She saved everything she had in order to give to others. One Christmas, she saved her money in order to buy Clifford his first instrument, even if it meant only having two dresses. Such was the character of Lenora Madsen.

Educational experiences were plentiful in the Madsen household. Lenora's focus on education was pervasive. She received a Bachelor of Science in Education degree from BYU later in life (1946), and a master's degree at age 60. Lenora taught her children to value their education and to respect their teachers. At the end of the day, she would often ask them: "What did you do to get the teacher to like you today?"

When Lenora met her future husband Charles at a teachers' convention, she said: "Someday I'm going to marry that man. I don't care if he's married and has half a dozen children, I'm still going to marry him some day."[5] She did in fact marry Charles, and they shared a long life together. Lenora had a major car accident in 1952. Thereafter, she suffered from headaches, loss of equilibrium, and a shift in her cognitive processes. She passed away in 1986 after a long bout with Alzheimer's disease.

Siblings

Clifford had 11 brothers and sisters (excluding baby Mabel, who died shortly after her birth): Myrtle (from his father's first marriage to Mabel), Lora, Mildred ("Millie"), Josephine ("Jo"), and Charlene (from his father's second marriage to Zina), and six others from his mother and father: Charley, Mary, Lenora ("Kaye"), Stanford, Carolyn, and Robert (Figure 1.8). Of those, Myrtle, Lora, Mildred, Josephine, and Kaye are deceased (as of 2016). Charlene is a retired private secretary and insurance clerk. Charley was a psychology professor at FSU before retiring, and he continues a private practice as a clinical psychologist in Tallahassee. Mary is a retired secondary school teacher.

Figure 1.8 Charles and Lenora Madsen with their 12 children. Top row: Charley, Clifford, Dad Charles, Mom Lenora, Stan, and Robert. Front row: "Millie," Charlene, Lora, Josephine/Jo, Myrtle, Mary, Carolyn, and Lenora "Kaye."

Stanford is a retired dentist. Carolyn works as an elementary and secondary substitute teacher. Robert is a clinical and forensic psychologist. Clearly, the family's focus on education persisted from the parents to the children.

The children were all taught to love and care for each other (Figures 1.9 to 1.11). Clifford remembers his mother asking him to walk his sister Kaye

Figure 1.9 Madsen siblings: Charley, Mary, Clifford, and Lenora "Kaye"

Figure 1.10 Clifford and brother Charley in 1942

Figure 1.11 Madsen siblings: Mary, Charlene, Mother Lenora, Charley, Clifford, Lenora "Kaye" in front

to school, letting him know that his first priority was to keep his little sister safe, holding her hand, never letting go, no matter what.

Mary Marakis

Clifford dated Mary Marakis (Figure 1.12) all through high school. Upon graduation and just before he attended Carbon College, he and Mary were married (17 August 1956). While Mary's mother was Danish, her father was Greek, and Mary was reared in the Greek Orthodox tradition. Clifford and Mary were married in Mary's home, and had a reception at the local Mormon Church to accommodate both families.

After marriage, Clifford and Mary lived in the school housing at Carbon College for two years until Clifford graduated. While attending Carbon College, Clifford worked for the Price Trading Music Company and directed the Helper City Bands. Mary worked as a telephone operator. They "half fondly" remember the two-room apartment where they lived. The walls were almost paper thin, and the rooms were heated by a coal stove in the

Figure 1.12 Mary Marakis circa 1991

kitchen and a potbelly stove between the living room and the bedroom. The stoves had to be stoked in the middle of the night on cold winter nights to last until morning.

Children

During their time in Provo, where Clifford attended BYU and worked in Heinselman's Music Store, Mary worked as a bookkeeper for a paint store until their first child, Sitka, was born (1959). Upon Clifford's graduation from BYU when Sitka was 18 months old, Clifford and Mary loaded all their belongings into a small U-Haul pulled by their Volkswagen and moved to Tallahassee, Florida.

With the help of Clifford's brother Charley, they were able to make a $500 down payment on a three-bedroom house, where they lived until their third child, Katia, was born (1968). They moved their larger family up the street two blocks, where they still live today. While Clifford attended FSU, Mary worked at the reception desk at the Duval Hotel until their second child, Cort, was born (1961). Mary then stayed home with her children while attending classes at FSU, eventually completing a Master's Degree in Education. When all three children were enrolled in school, she began teaching third grade at Caroline Brevard School and would later teach fifth grade. She taught there for 17 years.

All three of the Madsen children were given piano lessons, and each participated in musical programs in middle school and high school. Clifford believed that his children should all receive a music education just as they were expected to read and write. Sitka and Katia played the oboe, and Cort played the trumpet. All three children attended FSU, and eventually each earned a doctorate in their chosen field.

Sitka earned a M.S. degree in Audiology and Speech Pathology with a minor in Music Therapy, as well as a Ph.D. in Speech Pathology, at FSU. In 2008, she became a consultant for the Florida Division of Disability Determinations. As a consultant, she primarily reviews cases in which children with speech and/or language impairments are being considered for disability compensation. Sitka married Cartier Lammert in 1994. They live in Tallahassee and have two children.

At FSU, Cort completed an undergraduate degree in Biology, and then went on to earn a Master's in Molecular Biology (analyzing single-copy DNA to study the evolution of waterfowl) and a Ph.D. in Molecular Biophysics. Cort attended the University of Florida in Gainesville for four years to complete a post-doc in the field of mitochondrial genetics. After completing the post-doc, he continued his studies at the University of Virginia for three years, completing another post-doc studying phenotypic differentiation of vascular smooth-muscle cells and cardiovascular diseases. After his post-doc work, Cort accepted a position with Bristol-Myers Squibb developing drugs that target various cardiovascular diseases, and worked to discover drugs that treat heart failure. Cort married Melissa Alexandrowiecz. They lived in West Windsor, New Jersey, with their three sons until Cort's retirement in 2019.

Katia attended FSU, where she earned undergraduate and master's' degrees in music education. She taught middle school choir at Conway Middle School in Orlando, Florida, before going on to Louisiana State University to earn her Ph.D. Her first job in higher education was at Syracuse University in choral music education. After Syracuse, she accepted a position in the music department at Louisiana State University. Katia married Kent Del Castillo. They currently live in Raleigh, North Carolina, and have one son.

In rearing their children, it was Clifford and Mary's intention, like most parents, to instill a strong set of values. They wanted their children to value education and to be self-reliant. They wanted them to be honest and true to their beliefs, and to be tolerant and generous of means and spirit. In doing so, they supported each other in the decisions they made concerning their children's welfare and upbringing.

Notes

1. Chandler, Mary. *Lives of My Parents Charles H. Madsen Sr. and Lenora Roberts Kimball Madsen.* Unpublished manuscript. n.d.
2. Chandler, Mary. *Lives of My Parents Charles H. Madsen Sr. and Lenora Roberts Kimball Madsen.* Unpublished manuscript. n.d. P. 101.
3. Chandler, Mary. *Lives of My Parents Charles H. Madsen Sr. and Lenora Roberts Kimball Madsen.* Unpublished manuscript. n.d. P. 22.
4. Chandler, Mary. *Lives of My Parents Charles H. Madsen Sr. and Lenora Roberts Kimball Madsen.* Unpublished manuscript. n.d. P. 145.
5. Chandler, Mary. *Lives of My Parents Charles H. Madsen Sr. and Lenora Roberts Kimball Madsen.* Unpublished manuscript. n.d. P. 108.

2 Musical Beginnings

Clifford's early journey in music began with studying piano with Mrs. Allred, and later Mrs. Williams. Mrs. Williams's husband, Edgar "Toot" Williams, was Clifford's first elementary and junior high school band teacher. In the fourth grade, Clifford joined the tonette band, then moved to the Eb mellophone, the trumpet, and the French horn when he was in high school. Mr. Williams recognized his musical talent early on, and asked Clifford to march in the Pioneer Day parade with the high schoolers when Clifford was just in junior high school. He remembers this event as a highlight because he "got to wear a band uniform and march with all of those big guys" (Madsen, Clifford. Personal Interview. 29 June 2015).

He was the Harding Grade School drum major in the sixth grade (Figure 2.1). Many others in the school were aware of his musical talent. In fact, Clifford remembers that there was one year when the principal of his school learned that Clifford was thinking about quitting band.

> I went to another class, not band, and the principal all of a sudden comes to the door, he looks around and says, "Mr. Madsen," and I walked out . . . . "Why aren't you in the auditorium?" And I said, "I quit band." "No," he says. . . . "I want you to run home and get your horn and be back here before the bell rings."
>
> (Madsen, Clifford. Personal Interview. 29 June 2016)

In the middle of that year, a new student joined the band. Her name was Juanita, and she sustained his interest. Many of his students have heard Clifford tell the story of how he tried to woo Juanita with an overly affected Hispanic accent. His understanding of the social value of band, and the reasons why peer relationships can sometimes help kids choose to be in music programs, comes from firsthand knowledge. He stayed in band!

When Clifford was 15 and going into the ninth grade, Mary Marakis, his soon-to-be high school sweetheart, was in the eighth grade. Clifford recalls that "when I first noticed her I was absolutely smitten. I thought she was the most beautiful girl in the world. We started to date and then 'go steady'" (Madsen, Clifford. Personal Interview. 17 May 2019). The photo of Clifford in high school in Figure 2.2 references Mary, as Clifford was known to love "Greek salad . . . Greek girls . . . and music, music, music."

Figure 2.1 Clifford in sixth grade as drum major of the band

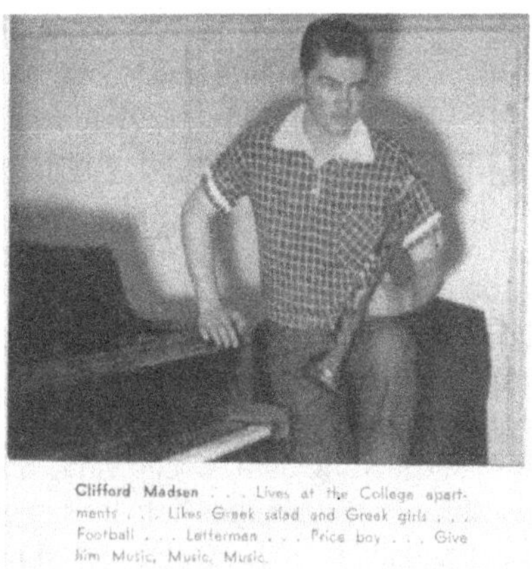

Figure 2.2 High school yearbook picture of Clifford

Clifford did not learn to read until he was in the third grade. His own recollections of learning to read and do math describe that the numbers and letters would "get all mixed up" (Madsen, Clifford. Personal Interview. 29 June 2015). No one really understood dyslexia at the time, and he struggled to overcome this obstacle during his school years. Later in his life, he was indeed diagnosed with dyslexia. He graduated eighth from the bottom of his high school senior class, and failed algebra three times. However, he was extremely active in extracurricular activities—on the debate team, on the football team (see Figure 2.3), in the chorus (Figure 2.4), as an actor in several plays (including *Antigone*), and, of course, in the band (Figure 2.5).

In high school, Clifford became involved in forensics, and later won several championships in debate and extemporaneous speaking. He attended Carbon High School, a campus that was at that time shared with Carbon Junior College. The school accommodated students who were in grades 11 and 12 and the first two years of community college.

As a very young boy, Clifford began to earn money any way he could. He tells the story about his first experiences as a babysitter. Clifford's older sister Mary had an outstanding reputation for babysitting, although one time when Mary was previously engaged, his mother sent him instead. His mother told him all of the rules for babysitting and ended with the admonition to

Figure 2.3 Clifford playing football at Carbon High School

Figure 2.4 Clifford as a member of the chorus (first row, second from the right)

Figure 2.5 Clifford and the Carbon High School/College Band

"do something a little extra," congruent with her values of a strong work ethic and generosity. In addition to his primary responsibility of keeping the children safe, she told him he should find a way to help in some other way. In his first real babysitting job, he noticed a huge stack of unwashed dishes, and washed them all while the children were asleep. Undoubtedly, word traveled quickly that Clifford was another of the Madsen children who was an excellent babysitter. Doing "something extra" became one of his core values while growing up.

Clifford held a number of jobs in adolescence. He remembers selling hot spud nuts (doughnuts made with potatoes) out of a truck, selling Cloverine Salve, stocking goods at a hardware store, setting up pins in a bowling alley, working as a janitor, delivering newspapers, and working at the Safeway grocery store and at Price Trading Company—a holdover from the old coal-mining days that sold everything from food to furniture to farming equipment, and included a music area that sold guitars, sheet music, pianos, and organs. When not busy, he amused himself by learning to play the Hammond Chord organ and other bigger organs that were sold to churches.

When Clifford was a junior in high school, his parents moved to Bountiful, Utah. Rather than moving to Bountiful with his parents, Clifford asked if he could stay in Price with his mother's best friend, Mrs. Wallace.

> Just before my entering tenth grade, my mother and father decided to move from Price, Utah to Bountiful, just North of Salt Lake. I definitely did not want to go. I was playing football, wrestling, debating, acting and, more importantly, going steady with Mary. I convinced my mother that I could be left in Price and live with one of her best friends, Ivern Wallace, the wife of a local mortician.
>
> (Madsen, Clifford. Personal Interview. 17 May 2019)

His parents eventually agreed, and Clifford stayed in Price until he married Mary, his lifelong partner and the love of his life.

Mrs. Wallace and her husband ran a mortuary, and Clifford stayed with them in a small apartment located on the top floor of the mortuary. Clifford recalled:

> The Wallaces lived in the same very, very large building that housed the Wallace Mortuary. The lowest floor consisted of the preparation room for the deceased, separated from the casket side of the lower floor where various caskets were displayed for subsequent purchase. The entire second floor was a chapel where we could hold funerals that accommodated up to 125 people. The third floor was the main home for the Wallaces and the very top floor was a small apartment which at one

> time was the bedroom, bathroom, and kitchen designed for their two older sons who were no longer living at home. This is where I lived for several years. It was convenient to my work at Safeway (a large grocery store chain in the West) and it was free!
>
> (Madsen, Clifford. Personal Interview. 17 May 2019)

Clifford learned a lot about the mortuary business while staying with the Wallaces, and still today, many of his thoughts about death are influenced by his time there:

> There were some important things I decided when living in the Wallace Mortuary. Even at 15, I decided that I was not going to attend funerals where the most important aspects were how many people attend and how important those people are that do attend. Or where people, many of whom do not even know the person, would go on and on about how wonderful the person was. I also decided to never retire, to donate my body to science, and to make sure that I visited loved ones before they died. One thing I learned very well when living there was when you're dead, you're dead.
>
> (Madsen, Clifford. Personal Interview. 17 May 2019)

In the place of taking a biology class in high school, Clifford worked in the local hospital laboratory doing blood counts, pregnancy tests, and routine lab work under the supervision of someone who had worked with Clifford's father during one summer when Charles was working as a soil tester at the nearby Scofield Dam. Clifford loved all of these jobs because of his unabated curiosity in most everything he did, which continues to this day.

Clifford supported himself rather well during those years away from his parents. When he was working at the Safeway grocery store, he would often bring home dented food cans that could not be sold, or meat that was nearly expired. Clifford was extremely resourceful and took care of himself. However, without his parents' supervision, he quickly found himself in trouble:

> Although I had come from a very wonderful family and thought I could manage very well by myself, I was wrong. It was at this time that I became more and more involved in dishonesties, including breaking and entering, stealing guns, etc. I was caught stealing gas from a school bus and had to appear before the Juvenile Court judge. My father had to drive down from Bountiful and I was put on probation. Actually, this crime was one of the least of my criminal activities and

> I always thought that I was "set up" by one of the football players on our team who did not like me. We were all getting gas from the school buses—as many as 6 to 9 of us got very good at siphoning the gas through a hose into a 5- or 10-gallon container. There were lots of buses parked during the night and the buses had large 50-gallon tanks. We did not think that they would miss a few pilfered gallons—and apparently they did not—at least for a long time.
>
> (Madsen, Clifford. Personal Interview. 17 May 2019)

While in high school, Clifford played in the Jimmy Dart Orchestra (Figure 2.6), a big-band community group made up of mostly adults that played "stock" arrangements at many of the area's larger events. His experiences there helped him to appreciate jazz and to learn how to improvise and to "swing" rhythms that differed in style from what he had previously learned. Clifford remembers the first time he played with the group and realized that he was not blending with the others. Jimmy told him, "Mr. Madsen, you know, nobody really plays the notes that are written. It doesn't matter if it is classical or jazz or whatever. You just use the notes as a guideline. But,

Figure 2.6 Jimmy Dart Orchestra. Clifford is fourth from the left in the back row

you know, in swing, you have to play it like this," and then demonstrated with brushes on the cymbal (Madsen, Clifford. Personal Interview. 29 June 2016). The adults in the group took him "under their wing" and helped him develop as a musician.

Alvin Wardle

Clifford has often said that in order to make it in life, one must get adopted. And not just once, but over and over. Al Wardle was Clifford's high school band director. Clifford says Al adopted him and literally saved his life. "Alvin Wardle is one of the biggest influences in my life, if not the biggest, outside of parents and family" (Madsen, Clifford. Personal Interview. 29 June 2016). But in listening to Al, you'd think it was the other way around! "Cliff always gave me a lot of credit and all I did was take care of a kid. He adopted us" (Wardle, Alvin. Personal Interview. 10 May 2016). Al's daughter saw so much of Clifford that she considered him a big brother. Clifford still goes to visit Al and his wife Beth about once a year. Al is retired in Logan, Utah. With only a nine-year age difference between Clifford and Al, they were and remain very close.

Al Wardle took the band director job in Price in 1954. That was about two years after Clifford's parents left for Bountiful in 1952. Price had always been a band town, and there were always parades and events that involved bands. At Homecoming, there would be 10–12 bands involved. Al had a huge job with not only the high school (grades 11 and 12) but the community college, and junior high programs in Wellington and Helper city schools. When Clifford began at Carbon College after high school graduation, Al approached the Superintendent of Schools, Mont Harmon, about getting some relief from his taxing teaching load. Mont Harmon was a Rotarian and knew Clifford (and Clifford's father) well from all of his nights of playing music at the Rotary Club meetings. Al suggested to Mont that Clifford teach the band at Helper Elementary School and Helper Junior High School, and Mont agreed. So, Clifford's career as a music educator began when he was just a community college student. He went to the two schools for one period each of band a day, then came back to take his coursework at the college.

Although Clifford was a trumpet player, Al needed someone to play the French horn. "I had other trumpet players, so Clifford became my first horn player. And, I just handed him the horn and said 'Here we go!' That's it!" (Wardle, Alvin. Personal Interview. 10 May 2016). Clifford also recalls that "he told me much later that he changed me to horn because he figured that I had talent but my brain or musical ear had long ceased to be connected to my musical output" (Madsen, Clifford. Personal Interview. 29 June 2016). He continued to play both instruments through graduate school.

Al really benefited from the fact that several of his students were in the Jimmy Dart Orchestra:

> That band was my nucleus. They were the kids that could play. And Jimmy had kept it going, despite his day job being a car parts salesman. So, I got kids in there that I had just enough kids to build a band.
>
> (Wardle, Alvin. Personal Interview. 10 May 2016)

When asked about his impressions of Clifford, Al said that Clifford was "bright, never pushy, outgoing, 'gung ho,' extremely talented, and never a 'smart aleck.' He just ingratiates you. And he is that way as a teacher. There was just an aura about him" (Wardle, Alvin. Personal Interview. 10 May 2016). He believed that one of the things that made Clifford so successful is "just plain commitment and belief in himself and belief in his mental processes . . . because he is organized and he is thorough" (Wardle, Alvin. Personal Interview. 10 May 2016). Clifford was also extremely curious. Al taught him how to repair instruments. Clifford was at Al's house, and Al took a metal clarinet completely apart—even all of the screws and levers—and asked Clifford to put it all back together. He did it flawlessly. These experiences helped him with his various side jobs in instrument repair.

Al tells the story of Clifford leading the band as drum major:

> Cliff was the drum major of the band proper. And Cliff showed up, I don't know where it came from, but we showed up for a parade and Cliff showed up with a big saber *(laughter)*. We developed a really good marching band. And I remember we did this parade in Provo and the only instructions I had given was for the kids to use the whole roadway. And so I wanted that width in the band. And so, those kids were going down the sides. Cliff gave them a pep-talk just before we kicked off and he just laid the law to them. Those kids came down the street, their eyes are up, not one head turned, they were just mesmerized. And, they had better be! And they were the best marching band I've ever seen. And the funny part was that I was, of course, following along like band directors do. And they were doing a great job. Max Dalby, from Utah State University, was the adjudicator. And, I remember Max got in behind the band. There was a big corner that we turned. A big column that we turned in Provo. And I didn't use a wheel turn, I used the only minstrel turn. So the guy breaks off on the right hand side and goes through the whole band, you never see, you never see anything. They pop out beside and it's a straight line. You don't see that lagging and all that stuff. Well, Max Dalby was adjudicating. And so he gets behind the

> band, we are coming to the corner, and he is watching for this and all of a sudden it's there, it's through, because it's such a clean turn.
>
> (Wardle, Alvin. Personal Interview. 10 May 2016)

Al was a true mentor to Clifford, and he worked hard to expose him to meaningful music experiences. For example, Al drove Clifford from Price to Provo every week to BYU to take trumpet lessons from Richard (Dick) Ballou. Dick was on the trumpet faculty and ran the marching band. Dick respected Clifford's work and recruited him highly for BYU. Al and Clifford took many road trips together, including to Eastman School of Music (in Rochester, New York), and to Los Angeles (to study with James Stamp, a trumpet player in the Philharmonic). They got to know each other very well during these road trips, and Clifford apparently practiced some of his skills learned in debate with Al:

> I know he was into speech and stuff like that. I think he did pretty well with that. Debate, he did that. In fact, I always resented that because he would debate me and I didn't know anything about debate. So, well, I never accepted . . . there is a pro and con. I could not understand how you could be against something and argue that point. Of course, I see it every day in politics now. Every day.
>
> (Wardle, Alvin. Personal Interview. 10 May 2016)

Some of those ideas of being able to state the pros and cons to particular viewpoints have remained with Clifford in his structure for his College Teaching class, where he asks his students to argue for and against critical issues in higher education in debate format. Usually, he will deliberately assign a position to the student he knows believes in the opposite viewpoint, to encourage intelligent thinking.

In an interesting turn of events where the teacher became the student, Al ended up going to FSU to work on his Ph.D. in Music Education with Clifford. With Clifford's help, Al finished the degree in 1968. Al was a classmate of Jayne Alley (now Standley) and Jere Forsythe. He remembers that Clifford "didn't let me get out of bounds. He was in charge!" (Wardle, Alvin. Personal Interview. 10 May 2016). Because everyone knew that Al had been Clifford's mentor, Clifford was always careful not to treat Al differently in class. Al's major professor was Jack Schwartz, who also served on Clifford's doctoral committee.

While Al was in Tallahassee, Clifford took him to Florida Agricultural & Mechanical University (FAMU), a historically black university, to watch their marching band. Al said that, coming from Utah, he had never seen that many people of color, and that it was one of his learning experiences with

Clifford, too. Clifford's desire to expand others' worlds and teach them to be comfortable with something outside of their experience has been a pervasive theme.

Al left Carbon College to work at Utah State University (USU). At that point, Carbon High School and Carbon College finally split. Al said that the faculty at USU actually wanted Clifford to take the job, but Clifford was working on his master's at BYU at the time because he was given the responsibility of directing the Cougar Marching Band. Fortuitously, the assistantship that Clifford did not take was made into a full-time teaching position given to Al. Al admits that perhaps he was not the greatest role model for Clifford in some ways, and may have led him astray once or twice: "I taught him one time, and I shouldn't have . . . but I taught him how to mix scotch whiskey with milk. Terrible, terrible! If I did some of those things now, I would be in jail!" (Wardle, Alvin. Personal Interview. 10 May 2016).

The College Years

Carbon College

After graduating from high school and struggling academically, Clifford continued on the same campus and began community college at Carbon College. That school has since been through two other names: College of Eastern Utah and, currently, Utah State University Eastern Campus. Clifford met Verda "Stubby" Peterson during his first week at Carbon College. Stubby had taught some of Clifford's siblings. According to Clifford, she adopted him when he first arrived:

> Nobody gets through life unless they are adopted two or three times, usually. Well, Stubby Peterson took it upon herself to adopt me, and she had me sit down and she grabbed my ear, and she was about as tall standing as I was sitting, and she grabbed my ear and she just twisted it and she said, "Now Clifford, you can't tell me that you are any stupider than your older brothers and sisters, and they are really smart, and I'm not going to have you not doing well. I want you to bring your homework here every day for me to check off." And I said, "Okay." And I did. So, from the very first week of college, I was a straight-A student from then all the way through.
>
> (Madsen, Clifford. Personal Interview. 29 June 2016)

From then on, Clifford was an excellent student, and graduated with high honors from Carbon College. In 2012, Clifford was awarded an honorary doctorate from that institution. He told the story of being adopted by Stubby Peterson in his commencement address.

After Carbon College, Clifford went to Eastman for a summer semester. Somehow (perhaps because he was with Al Wardle), he was assigned to take a graduate-level conducting course taught by Fredrick Fennell. During this class, the advanced conducting students got to conduct the Eastman Philharmonic Orchestra as their laboratory group. Clifford tells the story of how he studied his assigned piece diligently, going through each one of the parts again and again. During his time in front of this sophisticated group, he discerned that a particular ensemble member played a wrong note. Clifford addressed the situation by saying that he could not imagine how there was a misprint in the music. The orchestra member just smiled. Shortly later, another musician missed a note, and Clifford did the same thing he had done previously, blaming a misprint and not the musician. Later he realized that the orchestra was actually auditioning him, as they did most others in this group of "would be" conductors. Yet because Clifford did not react as did many others from the conducting class, who perpetually postured and claimed "hearing" more than they actually did, Clifford's naivete and honesty led him to become the "darling" of this group of auspicious musicians. After that first "audition," Clifford could do no wrong with this group.

Toward the end of that summer session, they finally figured out that Clifford was not a graduate student and quickly gave him an audition, whereby he was given a full scholarship to continue at Eastman as an undergraduate. However, Clifford left Eastman because he missed his girlfriend, Mary. He returned to Utah to continue his work with the Helper City Schools and graduated from Carbon College.

Brigham Young University

After graduating from Carbon College, Clifford enrolled in BYU. John R. Halliday, head of the music department, assigned himself to Clifford as his academic advisor. Dr. Halliday had received the first doctorate in music theory given at Eastman. He proceeded to ask Clifford what he had taken that summer while at Eastman, and upon hearing about Clifford's courses, Halliday decided that he did not need to take many additional courses at BYU. However, Clifford took additional courses, especially across all of the individual instruments, including violin, clarinet, and flute. His goal was to become as proficient on all of the instruments as possible. He played French horn in the University Symphony, and on several occasions he played the bass clarinet. He continued to play trumpet in the top university band, as well as in the Y's Men group. The Y's Men was a very selective, full big band that represented the university on many occasions, both in Provo and at other venues primarily used for recruiting.

Clifford stayed at BYU for his master's degree even though Max Dalby, Director of Bands at Utah State University, wanted him to come to Logan. Dick Ballou (who had taught Clifford private lessons beginning in high school through Al Wardle) was Director of the Cougar Marching Band and recruited Clifford to BYU. Dick left BYU that year to work on his doctorate at the University of Southern California. Ralph Laycock was the Director of Bands, and Clifford was well known throughout the department. At Laycock's suggestion, Clifford took over the marching band under Laycock's supervision. Laycock quickly determined that Clifford did not need much supervision, so he left Clifford alone after just a few visits. Clifford's assistantship was to direct the Cougar Marching Band and the ROTC band (Figure 2.7).

Clifford took a sociology class while at BYU that had a profound impact on him. For one of his assignments, he had to complete a socioeconomic scale, and various questions were asked related to his home life and living conditions. He could tell he was not doing very well on this test, but when he got to the very last question, he was asked to compute the number of "feet of books" in his house. He did not comprehend what "number of feet"

Figure 2.7 Clifford as director of the BYU Cougar Marching Band

meant, so he cautiously approached the instructor. “Did you have books in your house?” asked the instructor. “Oh yes, we have lots of books,” Clifford answered. “Well, estimate the number of feet across all bookshelves.” Based on that question, Clifford moved from lower-class to upper-middle-class status on the survey. The chair of the BYU sociology department approached Clifford after reading his term paper, and invited him to become a sociology major.

Clifford received the top graduate award from BYU and performed his master’s recital—half on horn and half on trumpet (see Figure 2.8).

BRIGHAM YOUNG UNIVERSITY
MUSIC DEPARTMENT

Dr. John R. Halliday, Chairman

Presents

CLIFFORD MADSEN
(Student of Ralph G. Laycock)

Carl Fuerstner at the Piano
assisted by Barbara Allen, Piano soloist

in

GRADUATE RECITAL
(No 112 in the 1959-60 Series)

Monday, August 15, 1960 - 8:15 p.m. - East Lounge Social Center

PROGRAM

Concerto for Trumpet .... Wayne R. Bohrnstedt
Briskly
Slowly
Spirited

Concertino for Trumpet .... Joseph Kaminski
"Un poco Vivaldi"
Improvisazione
Tarantella

Mr. Madsen

Prelude on a Gregorian Chant .... Ottorino Respighi

Miss Allen

INTERMISSION

Concert No. 1 for Horn .... Wolfgang Amadeus Mozart
Allegro
Allegro

Concert Etude Op. 49 .... Alexander Goedicke

Scherzo for Trumpet Op. 10, No. 1 .... Burnet Tuthill

Mr. Madsen

Figure 2.8 Clifford’s master’s recital program at BYU

Daniel Martino was his advisor, and he also worked with Harvey Fletcher, Sr. (best known for his work with the Fletcher Munson curves indicating equal-loudness contours for the human ear). Clifford conducted an experimental study for his master's thesis, exploring intonation differences with ascending versus descending scales. This thesis became his first publication in the *Utah Music Educators Journal*. Thus began a long love affair with research.

3 Career

Clifford's career at Florida State University (FSU) is a remarkable success story. He began as a doctoral student in 1960, and has been at the institution ever since, in some capacity. Throughout those nearly 60 years, he reinvented himself professionally numerous times, shifting his teaching focus from applied faculty member in trumpet, to band conductor, to his current position teaching research courses. His contributions in teaching, research, and service have been consequential and impactful.

Path to Florida State University

When considering where to go for doctoral work, Clifford initially thought he would attend the University of Kansas. He was particularly interested in the music therapy program there, and in possibly working with E. Thayer Gaston, as one of his BYU mentors, Daniel Martino, had done previously. However, because he did not have all of the anatomy prerequisites, he would have had to stay a much longer time. He also considered the University of Iowa. The main reason he chose FSU was because he could work on a doctoral degree while still performing and making music. He strongly believes in the philosophy that music educators are also musicians, and has built the music education program at FSU accordingly for his students.

> This is why I think it is absolute nonsense when you have the scholars over here and the conductors over there, the ties and the suits making fun of the turtlenecks over there who are making fun of the ties and the suits, and never the two shall meet. And it's not right. When people come to get their doctoral degree, they don't know if they are going to specialize in research or performance or both. And here at Florida State, in the three years they are here, they can follow whatever interests they have. And, a lot of people come in and want to be Director

of Choral Activities and they leave wanting to also teach choral music education classes.

(Madsen, Clifford. Personal Interview. 29 June 2016)

Clifford began working on his doctorate at FSU in 1960. His assistantship stipend was $1,500 per year, and tuition was not covered. His graduate teaching assistantship included teaching applied trumpet, baritone, euphonium, and other instruments with valves. Robert T. Braunagel was his supervisor.

His assistantship also included working in the Instrument Storage office, because of his background in instrument repair. When he first entered the instrument storage room, a number of instruments were off to the side, taking up space and considered junk. Clifford asked the Dean of the School of Music, Karl O. Kuersteiner, if he could be allowed to fix them and provide them to band programs in the Tallahassee area, which he did. Because he was new to the area, this decision started a long and very positive relationship with the state's public school band directors.

During his second year of doctoral study, Clifford's wife Mary got pregnant with their second child, Cort. They needed money. A job came open at Wakulla High School, and he told his supervisors that he would take the job so that he could earn some money. That is when he was offered a position as temporary instructor at FSU. As instructor, he was given opportunities to work with the Concert Band (see Figure 3.1), the Brass Band (Figure 3.2), the Symphonic Band (Figure 3.3), and the Marching Chiefs (Figure 3.4). Years later, band director Manley Whitcomb experienced a heart attack on the field while conducting the Marching Chiefs. Whitcomb approached Dean Kuersteiner to have Clifford fill in for him. In response to Whitcomb's request, Kuersteiner decided that Robert Braunagel should be given first choice to take over the Marching Chiefs. At that time, Braunagel was the trumpet teacher, but long before that, he had been the band director prior to the arrival of Whitcomb. Braunagel and Clifford were having a discussion late one evening, and he told Clifford that he was the band director when Whitcomb was recruited from Ohio State University. The budget for the marching band went from $500 to $10,000 under Whitcomb. Before saying yes to Dean Kuersteiner, Braunagel asked Clifford to help him with the marching band. Clifford said yes. That began a three-way partnership. Charlie Carter and Clifford were in charge of coordinating the music and halftime ideation for shows, while Braunagel directed the marching band and was responsible for charting. Both Clifford and Mary were very close to the Braunagels. Rosemary Braunagel loved to entertain their small children, Sitka and Cort, and provided many loving experiences across those years.

THE FLORIDA STATE UNIVERSITY

SCHOOL OF MUSIC

presents

ANNUAL SPRING CONCERT

The Concert Band

ROBERT T. BRAUNAGEL, *Director*
CLIFFORD MADSEN, *Associate Director*

Opperman Music Hall, Tallahassee
Tuesday Evening, February 25, 1964
8:15 o'clock

Figure 3.1 FSU Concert Band 1964 concert program cover

THE FLORIDA STATE UNIVERSITY

SCHOOL OF MUSIC

presents

Starlight Serenade

Brass Choir

CLIFFORD MADSEN, *Director*

Outdoor Theater, Tallahassee
Wednesday Evening, June 5, 1963
8:15 o'clock

Figure 3.2 FSU Brass Choir 1963 concert program

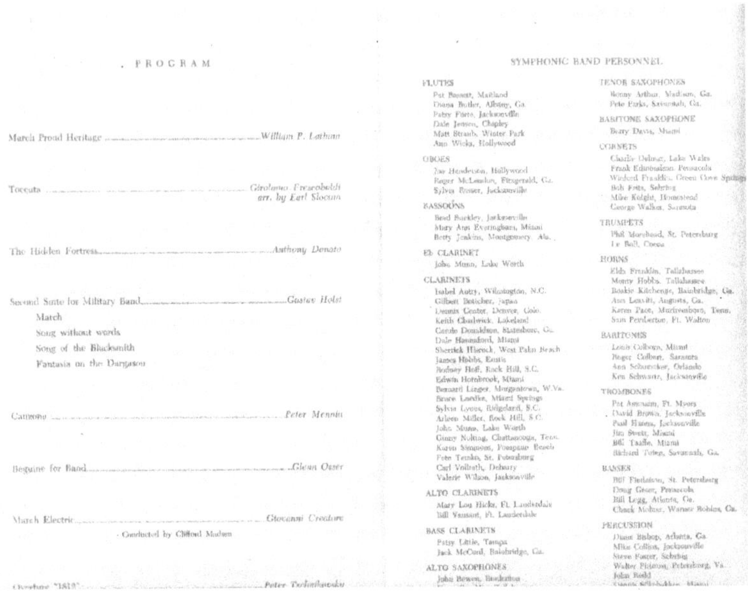

PROGRAM

March Proud Heritage .... *William P. Latham*

Toccata .... *Girolamo Frescobaldi*
arr. by Earl Slocum

The Hidden Fortress .... *Anthony Donato*

Second Suite for Military Band .... *Gustav Holst*
Match
Song without words
Song of the Blacksmith
Fantasia on the Dargason

Canzona .... *Peter Mennin*

Beguine for Band .... *Glenn Osser*

March Electric .... *Giovanni Creatore*
Conducted by Clifford Madsen

Overture "1812" .... *Peter Tschaikowsky*

SYMPHONIC BAND PERSONNEL

FLUTES
Pat Bassett, Maitland
Diana Butler, Albany, Ga.
Patsy Forte, Jacksonville
Dale Jensen, Chipley
Matt Straub, Winter Park
Ann Wicks, Hollywood

OBOES
Joe Henderson, Hollywood
Roger McLendon, Fitzgerald, Ga.
Sylvia Rosser, Jacksonville

BASSOONS
Brad Buckley, Jacksonville
Mary Ann Everingham, Miami
Betty Jenkins, Montgomery, Ala.

E♭ CLARINET
John Munn, Lake Worth

CLARINETS
Isabel Autry, Wilmington, N.C.
Gilbert Boticher, Japan
Dennis Center, Denver, Colo.
Keith Chadwick, Lakeland
Carole Donaldson, Statesboro, Ga.
Dale Hannaford, Miami
Sherrick Hiscock, West Palm Beach
James Hobbs, Eustis
Rodney Hoff, Rock Hill, S.C.
Edwin Hornbrook, Miami
Bernard Linger, Morgantown, W.Va.
Bruce Luedke, Miami Springs
Sylvia Lyons, Ridgeland, S.C.
Arleen Miller, Rock Hill, S.C.
John Munn, Lake Worth
Ginny Nolting, Chattanooga, Tenn.
Karen Simmons, Pompano Beach
Pete Tenkis, St. Petersburg
Carl Vollrath, Debary
Valerie Wilson, Jacksonville

ALTO CLARINETS
Mary Lou Hicks, Ft. Lauderdale
Bill Vassant, Ft. Lauderdale

BASS CLARINETS
Patsy Little, Tampa
Jack McCord, Bainbridge, Ga.

ALTO SAXOPHONES
John Bowen, Bradenton

TENOR SAXOPHONES
Bonny Arthur, Madison, Ga.
Pete Parks, Savannah, Ga.

BARITONE SAXOPHONE
Barry Davis, Miami

CORNETS
Charlie Delmar, Lake Wales
Frank Edmondson, Pensacola
Winford Franklin, Green Cove Springs
Bob Fritts, Sebring
Mike Knight, Homestead
George Walker, Sarasota

TRUMPETS
Phil Morehead, St. Petersburg
Lu Ball, Cocoa

HORNS
Eldo Franklin, Tallahassee
Monty Hobbs, Tallahassee
Rookie Kitchens, Bainbridge, Ga.
Ann Leavitt, Augusta, Ga.
Karen Pace, Murfreesboro, Tenn.
Sam Pemberton, Ft. Walton

BARITONES
Louis Colborn, Miami
Roger Colbert, Sarasota
Ann Schumacker, Orlando
Ken Schwartz, Jacksonville

TROMBONES
Pat Amman, Ft. Myers
David Brown, Jacksonville
Paul Hanna, Jacksonville
Jim Swett, Miami
Bill Taaffe, Miami
Richard Totten, Savannah, Ga.

BASSES
Bill Fiedelson, St. Petersburg
Doug Greer, Pensacola
Bill Legg, Atlanta, Ga.
Chuck Molnar, Warner Robins, Ga.

PERCUSSION
Diane Bishop, Atlanta, Ga.
Mike Collins, Jacksonville
Steve Foster, Sebring
Walter Fishman, Petersburg, Va.
John Redd

Figure 3.3 FSU Symphonic Band program

Figure 3.4 Clifford (second from the left) with members of the FSU band

Figure 3.5 Clifford's major professor Lew Pankaskie

Clifford considered Dr. Lew Pankaskie, a music theorist, one of the best teachers he had ever had (see Figure 3.5). He approached Lew about doing a dissertation using an experimental research method, based on the skills he had learned at BYU during his master's thesis. There had not been any experimental research studies conducted at FSU previously. Lew asked Clifford if he knew how to do an experimental study, and Clifford replied that he did. Lew became Clifford's major professor. Whitcomb, Jack Schwartz (music education), Donald E. Michel (music therapy), and Hugh Stickler (College of Education outside representative) were the other members on Clifford's doctoral committee. Later that year, Stickler, knowing that Clifford was an excellent teacher, asked him to teach the College Teaching course in the College of Education during the summer term.

Clifford believed that the fields of music education and music therapy needed experimental research. Several faculty members were not in favor of adding an experimental research class at FSU. FSU was known as a historical research institution at that time. Up until then, there were no empirical or behavioral texts specific to music, so Clifford wrote one. These events launched his textbook writing career.

FSU Teaching

Although Clifford began his career at FSU with teaching assignments in applied brass, then conducted band ensembles, he later transitioned into teaching music education and research coursework. He taught the following courses at the undergraduate level: Instrumental Methods, Elementary Methods, and Classroom Management. At the graduate level, he taught Developments in Music Education Curricula, Experimental Research in Music, Seminar in Contemporary Instructional Techniques, Behavior Modification in Music, and College Music Teaching. He taught both undergraduate and graduate Psychology of Music courses, including weekly laboratory experiences that his graduate teaching assistants coordinated. Clifford earned the title of Assistant Professor in 1964, Associate Professor with tenure in 1969, and Full Professor in 1973.

FSU Teaching Awards

Clifford has always loved teaching, and he has had both undergraduate and graduate classes every term since he began as a faculty member. His vita contains many accolades in recognition of his teaching. The most significant teaching award is the University Distinguished Teaching Professor, which he earned in 1990. This award is given only to those who have already received regular university teaching awards. All of these university teaching awards carry a stipend, and the most prestigious carries the title of University Distinguished Teaching Professor, a designation that lasts an academic lifetime. Clifford was in the first group of recipients of this award at FSU. Additionally, Clifford was among the first recipients of the Graduate Faculty Mentor Award and the President's Teaching Award. He received the Robert O. Lawton award in 1988, which is also a Distinguished Professor Award. Other awards include the Daisy Flory Parker Alumni Professor, and the President's Council for Excellence in College Teaching. His contributions to teaching at FSU have been remarkable.

Contributions in Music Therapy

Clifford became very interested in the field of music therapy, as it seemed a natural outgrowth of the work he was already doing. Additionally, it fit well with his desire to find tools to help others and measure effective protocols empirically. His work as a master's student with Daniel Martino at BYU, particularly regarding the influence of music on behavior, created in Clifford a strong desire to pursue scholarship and empirical study. Martino was a student of E. Thayer Gaston at the University of Kansas, and many consider Gaston to be the father of music therapy. When taking Don Michel's Psychology of Music class at FSU, Clifford discovered that the assigned text was Farnsworth's *The Social Psychology of Music*,[1] which was the same text he had in Martino's class at BYU. Thus began a long involvement with the field of music therapy that continues to this day. While in another of Michel's courses, Clifford went through the entire *Proceedings of Music Therapy* that included ten books containing all of the research in the field up to that time. These proceedings were the precursors of the *Journal of Music Therapy* that remains the premier journal in the field. At the same time, Clifford's brother Charley was completing his doctorate in psychology at the University of Illinois at Urbana-Champaign. Charley was affiliated with a group of students who had come to reject the traditional psychoanalytical positions of therapy, and identified with the new behavioral movement. Both Charley and Clifford were independently interested in the behavioral movement, which would later lead to an academic partnership resulting in the publication of *Teaching/Discipline: A Positive Approach to Educational Development*.

Even though Clifford was still teaching his regular instrumental music load, he approached Michel and said:

> Don, with your being the only person teaching the music therapy students, and considering that you are still performing violin with the string quartet, if you ever decide to give up any of the Psychology of Music classes, I'll be delighted to teach them.
>
> (Madsen, Clifford. Personal interview. 29 June 2016)

During the very next semester, Michel decided to have Clifford teach those classes, while he concentrated on the upper-level courses and the supervision of the music therapy interns.

In 1966, Clifford had a curious early interaction with E. Thayer Gaston at a music therapy conference that provides some context for his interest in the field and his behavioral thrust. Clifford shared this story with Barbara Bennett as part of the Baylor Oral History project (2000):

> [W]e had a conference—a National Association for Music Therapy Conference that I attended, and I gave a speech that was titled "Behavior Modification and Music Therapy." At that time my speech was given to the entirety of the music therapy community at the conference. Many years later, the group got big enough that we had concurrent

> sessions. Now you can have a three- or four-day conference and there will be five and six and seven things scheduled every hour. At that time we all met together in one great big auditorium. So, I had given my presentation and I was quite pleased with it. And I remember that E. Thayer Gaston got up, and as soon as he got up the whole room got absolutely quiet, and he said, "Well, behavior modification is good for rats and the retarded," and sat back down again. And so that was a bit of a punishment. . . . . And I got to know Vance Cotter (a doctoral student of E. Thayer Gaston's) at that conference. He sought me out and he said, "Oh, you don't have to worry about E. Thayer Gaston. Those guys are not behaviorally oriented." So I kind of took up with Vance. I mean, I understand now exactly why it was. I'd given this enthusiastic delivery and I was terribly punished, and when E. Thayer Gaston spoke, nobody else was going to say a word after that. Except Vance Cotter stands up and he says, "It's okay, it's okay, Cliff. It's okay to be a behaviorist."
>
> I became very close—not a close friend, but a close professional friend of E. Thayer Gaston much later on. And 20 years after that time, we sat down and visited as, I guess, scholars, at that particular point in time. And he discussed with me some of the feelings that he had had all the way back to some of those early times when he was taking me apart. And there was never anything personal, I think, with him. There was never any rancor. He was a person that was very strong and knew from his perspective what things were about and went about teaching others to think about that. But also, I never got any indication that there was any retribution or anything except good healthy disagreement. But as you might—well, I don't know if anybody thinks this but me, but it has always seemed to me that people at the very top of any kind of field of study seem to have a little bit more grace, a little bit more charitability, a little bit more perspective, generally, than the second, third, fourth, fifth echelons down the road, who kind of get to this issue of truth, where they learn the words but not the tune. And so I always felt that that was a good healthy interchange and exchange.[2]

Jayne Standley, who earned her bachelor's degree in 1966 at FSU, was a student of Clifford's in her undergraduate days in the Marching Chiefs, then later as a master's student in Psychology of Music and Behavior Modification. As a colleague of Clifford's serving on the FSU faculty starting in 1976, she had some context for Clifford's entrance and contributions to the profession. Prior to 1976, Don Michel was the Director of Music Therapy. FSU has only had two directors as of 2019—Michel and Standley. Jayne shared how, prior to Clifford, the majority of research and presentations in music therapy were not empirically or behaviorally oriented. When discussing whether Clifford could officially be considered a music therapist, Jayne shared that whenever the issue came up, others dismissed it due to the lack of an internship in the field:

> Because he didn't intern. Even though he worked with all those juvenile delinquent individuals on the side as volunteer work, nobody counted that as an internship. So, every time somebody thought Cliff deserved to be called a music therapist and would put his name forward people would jump up to say "He's not qualified," and yell and scream and all they would do is denigrate him because they believed he was divergent, taking us off in the wrong direction. That went on for years and years. People like Roy Grant would want to put him up . . . because you could become a music therapist through special means by demonstrating and volunteering for so many hours and by taking classes. Just by virtue of his research and his volunteering, there were people that wanted him to be called a music therapist. But it just would emotionally explode every time the subject came up. Some people felt that behavioral principles were not really music therapy. That's not really . . . right.
>
> (Standley, Jayne. Personal Interview. 23 June 2015)

In Clifford's interview with Barbara Bennett, he shared his experience about this issue:

> When I went to Florida State I took all of the courses that would be required for music therapy, and I spent a good deal of time working with agencies, including the juvenile court. And thereby, when it came time for me to become a registered music therapist—I could have become a registered music therapist had I wanted to count some of the things I was doing as an internship. At that time I did not think it was wise, and I remember speaking to Don Michel. Neither one of us thought it was wise for me to be a registered music therapist because of the courses that he was teaching and that I was teaching, and how we could parlay a little bit more work for ourselves, as far as the administration was concerned, by my not having the same credential as he. And to this day I am not a registered music therapist, which is really interesting because of the long association I've had with that group. And most people just assume that, of course, because that's the undergraduate registration that comes along with the baccalaureate at all the institutions and yet, that is something I didn't get involved with. And of course, from my perspective there was no need to. Don was there; there were other

> people, assistants that were coming back to do master's work that had the registration. That was not a big issue.
>
> Well, it became a little bit of a bigger issue when they decided they were going to change the requirements and grandfather in—as they say, grandfather, grandmother, grandperson in—all of the people who had been working in the field, but for whatever reason did not have registration. And of course, we have to remember this is a relatively young field even to this day. And at that point in time, I had people who—mostly former students from Florida State University, themselves registered music therapists—that first of all, it didn't occur to them that I was not registered. But when it did, they decided they would sponsor me, making sure that I would get through on this grandfather clause. Well, it was not as easy as they thought, because while there was a good deal of support for me, there was a good deal of non-support. And so for about two or three years my name would come up—I never wanted it to come up; I just wanted the thing to go away. But somebody, sure enough, would jump up on the floor of the general assembly and make the motion that Cliff Madsen be given this registration. Whereupon, somebody else would jump up, maybe because of my orientation or my sparring with E. Thayer over the years, or whatever, and say that they weren't comfortable with that at all. And so that was something that went back and forth for a good long while. It was more than a bit disconcerting and embarrassing for me.[3]

When asked to discuss Clifford's impact on the field, Jayne emphasized his extensive contributions to research:

> I think that he created the research base. He supported the journal and research sessions for 50 years as chair of research. He promoted the idea that research should be done and it was fun and it was a part of the profession. And he encouraged people to do research of all types. He invited those special speakers for research and there were always qualitative researchers in everyone. So, he created the research base for music therapy almost single-handedly, and then people became so intimidated there was only behavioral research and experimental research. There's always criticism.
>
> (Standley, Jayne. Personal Interview. 23 June 2015)

Carol Prickett and Alice-Ann Darrow were also early students of Clifford who pursued music therapy, and made rich and substantial contributions to the field in their teaching and their research.

Research

Establishing the Center for Music Research

When it was time to choose a major professor, Clifford was expected to choose Dr. Wiley Housewright, as everyone in music education had previously done. Housewright was a dedicated scholar who specialized in the history of music education practices in various education venues, especially those throughout the Southeast. Madsen did not want to do a historical dissertation, and wanted to do an experiment on intonation performances. This decision also had long-term implications regarding his shifting the research thrust of the profession from a historical approach to a more empirical approach. He had begun this study of intonation while completing his master's at BYU, and he wanted to do another larger study for his dissertation. As Dr. Housewright did not have that expertise, Clifford did not ask him to be on his committee. In his naivete, he did not think it would matter that much. Clifford chose Lew Pankaskie, who was a professor of music theory (see earlier in this chapter).

As Clifford began to get more and more involved in working with graduate students, several challenges had to be overcome related to teaching experimental research. At that time, Clifford was doing experimental research projects and helping several graduate students who wanted to investigate issues connected to experimentation. Clifford prepared a course proposal that was to go to the faculty for a vote. There was an undertow of some dissent concerning the course, and Clifford became concerned. When it was first presented at the faculty meeting, it was introduced by Joseph White, a long-time teacher of French horn and music theory. Professor White had befriended Clifford after Clifford had passed an inadvertent test given to him by White. One day when going into White's office, White put a sight-reading test in front of Clifford and asked him to read it. Thereafter, White befriended him, telling him that he considered Madsen a "musician," a word he said he did not use very often. It was after this test that Dr. White told Clifford that he could teach any of White's horn students, a distinction he heretofore allowed only for himself. Madsen already had more trumpet, euphonium, and tuba students than he could handle, but it was a nice gesture from Dr. White and Clifford appreciated it. Later, when White announced the proposal at the faculty meeting, Dean Housewright said, "Who will teach it?" After a notable silence, Professor White said that the question of who would teach any course was a separate issue, and White called for a vote. The vote was taken, and the proposal passed. Afterward, Clifford realized that White had taken some "lumps" for him. Thereafter, Clifford and White maintained a close friendship that lasted until White's death.

Development of the CRDI

One notable instrument for research that was developed at FSU was the Continuous Recording Digital Interface (CRDI). The CRDI's development began with a casual conservation Clifford was having with Jere Lee Forsythe. Forsythe, now retired from Ohio State University, was an original trumpet student of Madsen's; he entered FSU as a freshman when Clifford was teaching applied trumpet and studied with him throughout his entire undergraduate degree. Clifford often stated that Forsythe was one of the most musical and creative students he has ever had. When the Center for Music Research was established, it acquired the old facilities that had served as the FSU radio station for decades. Clifford appropriated a very small closet that previously had held all of the 10-inch tape recordings used by the radio station. This closet contained Clifford's "interesting devices"; they were interesting in their unusual nature. There was one piece of equipment that Clifford called his "James Bond device." It was a briefcase that camouflaged an inside recorder. With the tap of a small outside button, one could record a conversation and not be detected by the person being recorded. This special recorder was purchased when his former band teacher turned doctoral student, Alvin Wardle, came to FSU to get a doctorate. Wardle was interested in performance anxiety, and wanted to conduct an experiment in order to study it. He found that his participants were anxious and frightened with the visible tape recorder in the testing/treatment room. They all stated that if they did not have to see the device, it would be okay to have recordings made. Clifford began looking for such a device and found the "James Bond briefcase." Clifford has always said that he did not like most of the deceptions used in research, including any device or other aspects many researchers use in their work without the knowledge of the person being recorded or serving as a participant in a study. He preferred not to engage in deception.

Once when Jere and Clifford were looking for something in Clifford's closet of interesting devices, Jere noticed a round device that looked like a clock. He suggested that if that "clock-like" device could register data, it would be great for experiments. Building on that idea, Clifford enlisted the help of E.T. Kawaguchi, a gifted technician at the Center for Music Research who developed the beta version of the CRDI. At that time, the CRDI had two forms; one used a lever moving on top of a shoe-like box. and the other used a clock-like device. The box was easy to design, while the round CRDI proved more problematic. Charles (Chuck) R. Robinson was a doctoral student during that time, and was working part-time for a Tallahassee glass repair company. He suggested making a hard plastic support that would accommodate various overlays for experimental purposes, attached underneath by the small potentiometer that could record voltage fluctuation from movement of the dial developed by Kawaguchi. Thus, the finished device looked much like clocks today that have a small device attached through a hole that registers time. Robinson and Earlene Rentz Turner, also a doctoral student, produced the first two studies using the CRDI (which was named by Robinson) for their dissertations. Earlene used the box to study focus of attention to instrumental families during Aaron Copland's *Billy the Kid*. Robinson used the round CRDI to study listening patterns in choral music. Since its inception, it has been used in over 100 research studies investigating focus of attention, musical tension, aesthetic responses, intonation, rubato, expressivity, tension, and even teacher characteristics such as pacing and teacher intensity.

Research Awards in the Profession

In addition to his teaching awards, Clifford has earned numerous awards that recognize his research contributions in the fields of music education and music therapy. He was the first recipient of the Publications Award, given to him by the National Association for Music Therapy. This organization (later renamed the American Music Therapy Association, or AMTA) also granted him the Award of Merit, the Presidential Award for Outstanding Contributions to the Field of Music Therapy, the Lifetime Achievement Award, the Presidential Citation (special recognition for 50 years of continuous refereed research presentations at the national conferences of the AMTA), and the Presidential Award for Extraordinary Committee Leadership, having served on the Research Committee from 1976 to 2011.

Clifford's international contribution to the profession is vast. He was the first life member of the International Society for Music Education (ISME) Research Commission, and received a Lifetime Achievement Award from the organization. Additionally, he received the Lifetime Achievement Award from the Society for Education, Music, and Psychological Research (Sempre). The World Federation of Music Therapy awarded him the outstanding Music Therapy Pioneer Award for establishing one of five international models of music therapy.

In the field of music education, Clifford was the first recipient of the Senior Researcher Award, an award given by the Music Educators National Conference (now the National Association for Music Education, or NAfME) biannually to a leading researcher in music education who has sustained a record of scholarship across a lifetime. Similarly, the Music Educators National Conference Hall of Fame and the Lowell Mason Award recognized Clifford's contributions to both teaching and research on a national scale in the profession.

In his Senior Researcher acceptance speech, Clifford said, "Perhaps someday research will be so valued in the music community that researchers will state proudly one of Cornelia Yarbrough's phrases, '*Research* is my performing instrument.'"[4] Indeed, for Clifford, research has been his performing instrument for many years.

Service

Clifford has often stated that it is important to serve in professional organizations, and that one can likely only be a meaningful active member in two organizations. In his career, consistent with his professional identities, he has served the music education and music therapy organizations across his lifetime, in an impactful and generous way. Notably, he has served on the research editorial boards of eight journals: *Bulletin of the Council for Research in Music Education* (1990–2009), *International Journal of Arts Medicine* (1991–2002), *International Journal of Music Education* (2010–2016), *Journal of Band Research* (1982–1996), *Journal of Music Therapy* (1974–2000), *Psychology of Music* (1989–1997), *Journal of Research in Music Education* (1970–1976, 2000–2006), and *The Quarterly: Teaching and Learning in Music* (1991–1997). Additionally, he has served as a guest reviewer for the journals *Perceptual and Motor Skills*, *Psychological Reports*, and *Research Studies in Music Education.*

Clifford's other service in research outside of editorial committee work has included positions on the Music Education Research Council (MERC) for the Music Educators National Conference (2008–2014), with leadership as Chair in 1982–1984; Chair of the National Research Committee for NAMT-AMTA for 35 years (1978–2013); and the Society for Research in Music Education (SRME) in 2010.

At FSU, he assumed the Coordinator role of Music Education/Music Therapy/Contemporary Studies in 1977, and has held that position ever since. He was on the University Senate from 1965 to 2019. His record of service on the University Steering Committee over 50 years was remarkable, and was recognized by FSU in the form of a citation. It appears below:

> Special order: Special Recognition April 22, 2015 Faculty Senate Presentation, Gary Tyson
>
> Whereas, Senator Clifford K. Madsen joined the Florida State University faculty senate in 1965 and has served as a member of the senate continuously for a period of 50 years; and
>
> Whereas, during that time, Clifford K. Madsen has served on virtually every sub-committee of the senate including 39 years on the senate steering committee; and

Whereas, Clifford K. Madsen has been an unwavering voice in support of faculty governance, and through his efforts, has helped build many of the traditions and structures of the current senate; and

Whereas, Clifford K. Madsen has demonstrated an unparalleled record of service excellence to the university and the faculty senate;

Therefore, be it resolved that the faculty senate of the Florida State University hereby recognizes and commends Clifford K. Madsen for his unfailing commitment to the betterment of our university for these past many years and celebrates his continued service in his 51st year on the FSU faculty senate.

Clifford served FSU in countless ways, through the Faculty Elections Committee, search committees for major administrators of the university, the Faculty Honors Committee, Academic Affairs committee, Graduate Council, Admissions Committee, Minority Affairs committee, Equal Employment Opportunity committee, University Promotion and Tenure committee, University Council on Teaching, and University Budget committees, among many others. He was proud to be a founding member of the Board of Governors for the University Center Club (1996–2007), the group that established a restaurant inside the FSU football stadium which facilitated a partnership and employment opportunities for students in the hospitality major.

Clifford's work in his own state was never secondary to his national commitment in music education. The Florida Bandmasters Association inducted Clifford into the Hall of Fame in 2015. The Florida Music Educators Association inducted Clifford into the Hall of Fame in 2011. Moreover, his commitment to the community is evidenced by early work in a juvenile detention center for ten years, working as a juvenile court counselor under Leon County Judge Rufus D. Jefferson from 1963 to 1973.

In the three areas of teaching, research, and service, Clifford has been a model faculty member at FSU for over 50 years. Please visit www.cliffordmadsen.com to see a complete list of his publications, presentations, and service.

Notes

1. Farnsworth, Paul R. *The Social Psychology of Music*. Oxford, England: Dryden, 1958.
2. Bennett, Barbara. *Oral Memoirs of Clifford K. Madsen*. Institute for Oral History. Baylor University, 2000. Pp. 67–73.
3. Bennett, Barbara. *Oral Memoirs of Clifford K. Madsen*. Institute for Oral History. Baylor University, 2000. Pp. 73–75.
4. Madsen, Clifford K. "Senior Researcher Acceptance Address." *Journal of Research in Music Education*, vol. 88, 1988. P. 138.

Part II

Philosophy

A Love of Learning

4 Philosophical Tenets

> "What is your philosophy?"
> "Behavior is true."
> "What behavior?"
> "All behavior including thoughts and everything else."

Clifford Madsen had a passion for philosophy from a very early age. His mother presented him with a book in his early teen years, *The Story of Philosophy: The Lives and Opinions of the Great Philosophers of the Western World* by William Durant.[1] Inscribed on the inside cover of the book were the words, "To Clifford, you were always our little philosopher." Clifford later joked that "one should never gift a book that one has not read for oneself" (Madsen, Clifford. Personal Interview. 17 May 2019), as that book inspired him to reconsider many aspects of life, including his faith and participation in the Church of Jesus Christ of Latter-day Saints. To his family's disappointment, his philosophical journey ultimately led him to leave the Mormon Church.

> I grew up in a very large family, all of whom were or appeared to me at that time to be ardent Mormons, i.e., the Church of Jesus Christ of Latter-day Saints. Indeed, I was a "true believer." I remember during seventh grade dreaming of converting thousands of people to the "true LDS faith."
>
> Reading that book (*The Story of Philosophy*) literally changed my life. Since that experience I have told people to never give anyone a book that they have not read themselves. If my sweet mother had thought that by my reading that book it would sow the seeds that would eventually lead to my leaving the church, I am sure she would have never given it to me. However, it was much later when I was the Director of the Marching Band at BYU that I finally came to the realization

> that I did not have a "testimony," as the Mormons would say. For me, deciding if the church was the only true church was important. It mattered to me; it mattered a lot. I remember many times going up into the mountains just outside of Provo and ardently praying to find my way. At that time the church did not allow persons of color to hold the Priesthood. Furthermore, women then, as now, were and are supposed to be subservient to their husbands. I found both positions antithetical to my concept of what a deity would advocate.
>
> (Madsen, Clifford. Personal Interview. 17 May 2019)

To this day, Clifford frequently references the early philosophers. His philosophical orientation influences his personal life, teaching life, and research life. He truly embodies and lives the values that he espouses, and these values include empowerment/individual choice, making decisions based on data, a positive behavioral approach, transfer, pursuit of happiness, and that time is life.

At the forefront of Clifford's philosophy is the empowerment of the individual. He empowers those around him by teaching independence and a sense of personal responsibility. Clifford is known for his behavioral approach, which provides the underpinnings for many of his authored books: *Applications of Research in Music Behavior*, *Research in Music Behavior*, *Teaching/Discipline*, *Experimental Research in Music*, *Competency-Based Music Education*, and *Contemporary Music Education*. In fact, he coauthored many of these books with his students as a way to empower them as thinkers and scholars. While some may associate behaviorism with a teacher-centered approach—wherein the teacher wields power and control—Clifford teaches individuals that they are responsible for their own lives and have the ability to make their own choices. "Maybe this goes all the way back to my dad and his concept of free will, but . . . to me, my intervention with students almost entirely is to help them do what it is that they WANT to do" (Madsen, Clifford. Personal Interview. 26 June 2015).

Empowerment/Individual Choice

In order to become empowered, one must first realize that one has the ability to choose and take control of one's life. Clifford encourages those around him to consider the ability to choose, and to value the subsequent learning that occurs when one makes a choice. In *Teaching/Discipline*, one portion of a chapter is devoted to "Who Decides Who Decides."[2] He suggests that individuals, in many cases, are unaware of which choices they have made for themselves, compared to the choices that have been made for them.

> I mean, how does one go about choosing? Take the kid in the ice cream store and you need to get the biggest one that you can have with the most flavors and you say, "Get whatever you want." Then the next time you come in, you can say, "You can have anything except the one you got last time." And after you're convinced that you're getting bored out of your mind because you're only on flavor 23, say, "Okay, get whatever you want." But for most people, ice cream is chocolate. They either like it or they don't, and then from then on, they think that they chose chocolate. You didn't choose chocolate, it chose you.
> (Madsen, Clifford. Personal Interview. 19 June 2015)

How does one know whether one has chosen something if multiple options were never explored? The point of the story is that many of us fail to recognize the fact that much of what we do and what we believe does not come about because we carefully consider multiple options and then make conscious choices among them. Rather, in many dimensions of our life experience, we never really know about or consider all of the available possibilities, and thus make no real choice at all. The ice cream story can be extended to any concept, idea, ideology, religion, and so on. "And one of the things that bothers people in my class more than anything else is when I say, 'Think of something that you've always believed in and then ask, when did I have a choice?'" (Madsen, Clifford. Personal Interview. 19 June 2015).

By sharing the ice cream story, Clifford wants people to reflect on the unconscious choices they have made without considering alternatives, and then consider carefully what they believe, what they do, and what they think. One powerful lesson he shares with students is the concept that we can choose what we replay in our own minds. During Clifford's time at BYU, he wrote a sociology paper that told the story of two very different people. The essay outlined what would become one of his main philosophical underpinnings. He presented the concepts from this essay many times at various conferences. Below are the excerpts transcribed directly from his 2015 keynote to the Florida Music Educators Association, which he entitled "Diversity in Thinking"[3]:

> This presentation is based on two different situations: The first describes a student who is extremely poor and has a difficult life; the second describes a student who has had a very fortunate life. . . . I'll call the first one Stan and the second student Robert. Stan comes from a big family and both his parents must work to support all of their 12 children. Stan knows he is poor because of many things. Stan wears old clothes, most of them are hand-me-downs, from someone else or bought used from Goodwill, and some are gifts from his church. Robert

wears clothes that he thinks are really cool, because most come from his older brother.

Robert goes to lunch every day with his friends and has a great time hanging. Sometimes Stan does not have money for lunch and it embarrasses him to tell anyone. In fact, Stan is often embarrassed about being poor. Stan wants a new pair of sneakers, but his mom tells him there is no money. There never seems to be any money.

Stan says, "At Christmas, I never got a present. Only my little brothers and sisters got a present. I only got an old washed out nylon sock filled with apples, oranges, and hard candy." Robert says, "I just *love* Christmas morning. Everyone comes into the front room in a single file starting with my littlest sister. We all watch her as she opens her special gift. She is so cute! It makes us all very happy."

In the first grade, Stan has a terrible stuttering problem. Everyone tells him to slow down and think about what he wants to say, but they just don't understand. It's so hard to do. Robert gets along with almost everyone and he thinks that some teachers like him. Robert's older brothers and sisters take good care of him.

Stan has difficulty with schoolwork. All the numbers and letters get all mixed up. They send him to take lots of tests. It takes him until the third grade to start to learn how to read. Stan is also very heavy for his age. He weighs over 150 pounds in the fifth grade. Other boys make fun of him and call him "Roundy." Stan wants to play basketball, but he is way too slow to run up and down the court fast. He also is not good at baseball and prays that the ball will not come to him because he is afraid he will drop it.

Robert starts playing football in the eighth grade. He is great at blocking and tackling. In high school he makes the first team and gets a letterman's jacket with the big high school letters on it.

Stan wants to play trumpet in the school band, but he knows that his parents cannot afford to buy or even rent an instrument. Robert asks the school band director if the school owns any instrument he can play. He has an old rusty horn, but he loves playing it.

Stan fails algebra three times. All of his grades are not very good. He cannot make the college track but finally graduates eighth from the bottom of his big high school class in the general track intended for those not going to college. Robert is in band, chorus, acting, debate, and still plays football through high school. Robert thinks maybe he can get a scholarship to go to college doing some of those things.

Almost everyone Stan knows goes to work in the coal mines. It's hard and dirty work, but it pays really well. One of his friends who graduated one year earlier bought a really cool new car. When Stan is 15, his family moves away and leaves him with his mother's friend. Stan gets in trouble and is stealing from a lot of different places. He finally gets caught stealing gas from a school bus.

Robert at age 15 has three different part time jobs to earn money. He enjoys the grocery store where he quickly progresses from bag boy to produce manager. But his favorite job is a music store where he learns to play lots of different instruments.

So how do you think Robert turned out?
What about Stan?

Now I will tell you that Stan and Robert are the very same person and I am that person. Stan and Robert are the names of two of my brothers. I'll bet that everyone here can tell my same two stories: one really bad, leaving out any of the good, the other very good leaving out most of the bad.

The latest research indicates that we live inside our heads and what becomes real to us is whatever we choose to think about. We can rehearse mostly the bad, or we can decide to dwell on the good. For example, I played and conducted many, many concerts in my life. I can choose to rehearse in my mind the good ones, or I can choose to rehearse the few missed notes in an important performance. That awful time I got lost as a conductor. Those thousands of times that, if I think about those missed notes, it becomes my REALITY, now. Not then.

Rehearsing events in one's mind is a habit that can be counterproductive, particularly when the individual replays negative events. The repetition of the negative perception can take on a life of its own when replayed over and over, thus becoming a new reality or truth for that individual. The hurtful event is played again and again, and through this process the individual is inadvertently punished. Some psychologists refer to these negative repetitive thoughts as rumination. Choosing to hit rewind and replay a positive event has the ability to empower the individual to become who they want to be, rather than fixating on the negative. Clifford Madsen believes that we have the ability to choose what we replay, and that we can focus primarily on replaying the positive. Focusing on positive interactions, choosing things that make us happy, and responding to others with kindness, embody much of Clifford's philosophy.

A (Positive) Behavioral Approach

How Clifford came to choose a behavioral approach and align himself with behaviorism is an interesting story. First, he grew up in a household with 12 children, and both of his parents were educators with reputations for being extremely adept at classroom management. In fact, in the opening of the *Teaching/Discipline* book, the acknowledgement reads, "To our parents—lifelong teachers, unwitting behaviorists, wonderful people." Clifford's father was a principal of Price city schools for 32 years. His mother was a fifth-grade teacher and had the reputation of being able to work successfully with students who had behavioral challenges.

> And I think that I discovered what she did. The thing that she would do is just get these little kids to love her, any way she could and as quickly as she possibly could. And I mean that in the true sense of love. And once they did, and of course, that was in some cases easy and in some cases difficult, but once they did, then she'd use that to teach them.[4]

The idea of building relationships and reinforcing those around you was taught to Clifford from an early age:

> My mother used to always ask me when I went to school—the first day of school, she said, "Well, what are you going to do, Clifford, to get the teacher to like you?" And I didn't know what I was supposed to do, but I knew what the charge was. And so, I'd go to school every time just waiting for whatever the opportunity was to get that teacher to like me. And that was just one of her many techniques, things that she'd do—setting up expectations, of course. And I'd come home after the first day, and she'd say, "Well, what did you do, Clifford?" And I'd say, "Well, I don't know, but when the teacher said, 'Everybody line up,' I lined up and did those things." And she said, "Well, that's good. You just keep trying."[5]

Clifford's affinity for a behavioral approach was not immediately tied to the philosophy or writings of B.F. Skinner, as many may have assumed. Rather, he was aware of the behavioral movement in the mental health field that occurred simultaneously with his early years teaching college at FSU. At the time, Ullmann and Krasner had written *Case Studies in Behavior Modification*.[6] In an interview with Clifford, he recalled:

> Ullmann and Krasner were doing research where they would take these people who had no self-skills at all and they would put them in these behavior programs. First of all, instead of having them just eat

> whenever they wanted to eat, they would take lunch and truncate it, truncate it, truncate it, and then they would just lock the door.
>
> (Madsen, Clifford. Personal Interview. 19 June 2015)

In the study referenced, the patients were taught independence, self-help, and social skills by using mealtime as a reinforcer.

> So, if you were there in an hour, you got to eat. If you weren't there, then they didn't let you in. You just had to wait until the next meal. So, then they started to give people keys so they would have to unlock something to get into the lunch room. But the keys would only unlock if you coordinated with another person . . . if I am remembering this correctly. . . . So then, in order to eat, you would have to get a buddy that would come with his key to open it at the same time you are opening it. They had to communicate. And they started from absolutely no communication or self-help skills and they taught the patients to communicate and interact. And, it was the whole revolution of mental health. And actually, teaching people to do what, up to that point in time people thought was just not possible. So that's how I got into it [behaviorism].
>
> (Madsen, Clifford. Personal Interview. 19 June 2015)

Another key experience that further developed Clifford's behavioral views were his ten years of experience working with juvenile court cases. He tells the story of how he decided to serve the Tallahassee community in this capacity.

CM: I came by these things by, you know, what I was doing face to face with the juvenile court kids.

RM: So, how did you end up getting involved with the juvenile detention center?

CM: That was a better story than most of the others because, here I was . . . you know . . . easily, easily could have been put in prison. I mean, I was breaking and entering and stealing firearms. They eventually caught me stealing gas out of a school bus . . . so, when I got here (FSU) I said, well, I really need to be giving back to the community. So, the first thing I thought of was scouting because my dad was a Silver Beaver and I was the youngest Eagle Scout in the State of Utah. Important stuff . . . and then I went out and found out that all of those scouting kids needed somebody but not me. And I thought, "Well, where do they need somebody?" Juvenile court. Why? Because I had been there. Done that. I had worked in a prison. I had had all of those experiences. So, I went down to the court and I said, "I want to serve." And they said, "Fine." So, I apprenticed very quickly through

> this, that and whatever. And I finally got to the point where the judge would give me the most difficult cases and only those (individuals) that were sentenced.
>
> (Madsen, Clifford. Personal Interview. 19 June 2015)

The research case studies, his personal upbringing, and his experience working in the juvenile court influenced his philosophy. *Teaching/Discipline: A Positive Approach to Education Development*[7] was a translation of the behavioral approach used by the mental health community into the classroom. Two elements delineated the *Teaching/Discipline* book, and more importantly Clifford's philosophy, from what was going on at that time: 1) Empowering the individual by engaging them in the interventions through self-shaping, including thoughts as behaviors; and 2) transferring the positive behavioral approach into the music classroom environment.

Cognitive behaviorism recognizes thoughts as behaviors because thoughts can be observed, recorded, and analyzed by the individual to whom they belong. This approach deviates somewhat from the foundation of behaviorism, which did not originally recognize thoughts as behaviors. This perspective, or shift in ideology, cannot be overlooked, as it is the inclusion of thoughts in the behavioral approach that empowers the student or client.

Transferring the primarily positive approach into the field of music education and music therapy was another contribution made by Clifford. Participants who attended his clinics or were enrolled in his courses will recall the recommended ratio of four approvals to one disapproval for effective teaching. While Clifford was not the originator of this educational research, he produced a number of studies that contributed to the research literature in this area. He also modeled using a predominantly positive approach in his courses and social interactions. Throughout his career, Clifford developed numerous observational tools to empower teachers to review their interactions with students, such that they are able to transform their teaching and realize their personal goals.

Making Decisions Based on Data

If behavior is true, and behavior is anything that can be observed directly or indirectly, then it can be recorded and measured. By asking questions, researching information, and collecting data, one can make informed decisions. Making decisions based on data transfers directly back to the individual's ability to choose. If each of us has the ability to choose, on what basis ought that choice be made? Clifford emphasizes making decisions based on data. When asked what his main goals are for his students and loved ones, he shares, "I want people to become more empirically oriented. The main thing that I try to get across, I've never been that successful with, and that has to do with using the benefits of research to inform your life" (Madsen, Clifford. Personal Interview. 19 June 2015).

One of the first lessons Clifford teaches those interested in conducting research is a clear delineation between three approaches to research: phenomenological, assumptive, and hypothetical. These three approaches are outlined in his *Experimental Research in Music Workbook*.[8] He stresses to his students that when one believes in something—in essence, has found a personal truth—gathering information for the purpose of supporting what one already believes is dishonest, and corrupts the integrity of the research process. Using this type of approach is assumptive. You assume you already know the answer, and simply attempt to defend your point of view. Contrast the assumptive approach to a hypothetical approach where the individual asks an honest, open question, collects data to find the answer, and accepts the outcome of the research regardless of their previously conceived notion.

> I use the model about three different ways of the experimental, the phenomenological, the assumptive—and that has proven to be very useful and concise. And, a lot of things you throw away or you make them better, but that one little model of: What is experimental and what is not? What's the enemy? Well the enemy is the assumptive. "I know what truth is and I will just keep looking for the truth that I already know to be true." And, people who really get that and really worry about it start to think a lot and come up with questions like, "Gee, almost everything is assumptive, isn't it?" "Yes, it is." And, you know, it's going to change in the light of systematic inquiry, i.e., research.
>
> (Madsen, Clifford. Personal Interview. 26 June 2015)

Clifford uses data to inform the majority of his decisions, including those related to his research, teaching, and personal life. Here is an example of one way that he uses research to inform his teaching:

> That is another study I did. People say, "Well, I want to come and check and see (my grades) because I can't remember if I did that (assignment)." So, I thought, "Okay, that is a legitimate point of view. Let me see if that is true."
>
> (Madsen, Clifford. Personal Interview. 19 June 2015)

So Clifford collected data on 200 or so individuals, and found that:

> Everybody knows what they missed. And when they come in to ask me, what they are really saying is, "Did you catch this one that I didn't do?"

> So . . . you know, instead of sitting for 50 years saying, "I wonder if that is really true or not. . . ." Somewhere, 35 years ago I said, "Well, okay, give them the benefit of the doubt—start taking data. Take data for a year or two and get up to three or four hundred and you haven't found your white crow yet or your black swan."
>
> (Madsen, Clifford. Personal Interview. 19 June 2015)

The reference to a white crow or black swan is a research reference. There is no way to prove that white crows do not exist, so one simply continues to look for an exception because it may exist. The concept also has implications for testing of null hypotheses. Through his data collection process, he found that his students were very aware of which assignments they had completed, and which they had not. He was unable to find a "white crow," an individual who sincerely was unaware of which assignments had not been completed. By repeatedly using data to make decisions, he came up with a system for grading, providing feedback, guiding undergraduate research, and so on. The point here is not what decisions he made, but rather that his decisions were not made arbitrarily. They were made based on evidence. Making informed decisions is something that he tries to teach his students and loved ones. "Research is a *modus operandi*, a method by which we can organize actions to be consistent with our thoughts and test these actions intelligently, realizing that through thoughtful trial and error we can better ascertain the worth of our ideas."[9]

Transfer

Transfer, the ability to take an idea or concept from one context and understand or recognize that same idea in another context, is at the center of Clifford's teaching philosophy. A common phrase that he utters is, "Everything relates to everything." Teaching for transfer permeates all teaching and interaction with Clifford. The beginning of every one of his classes is devoted to 5 minutes of a transfer writing activity. He frequently points out that the majority of individuals do not transfer information automatically, without prompting. And, without the ability to transfer, it becomes difficult to learn independently.

> The first time I thought about transfer was from a philosophical point of view. I say this all the time, but my favorite story, that I should tell more often, is that when you're a little kid, it seems like you have hours to observe. I mean every day is like a century or two, especially if you're bored. So, you sit there and start to observe. You've got a window, and you've got a screen, and you've got a fly in there (trapped) and you say,

> "Where'd that fly get in there?" Then you look down and you see this little hole. And you think to yourself, "You know, fly, if you approached this systematically, you would eventually get out." Flies have 1,000 eyes or whatever it is. It's not that they can't see; they see really well. So, that's when I realized that the most important thing that education should do is to teach people how to use knowledge.
>
> (Madsen, Clifford. Personal Interview. 19 June 2015)

One of Clifford's main educational goals became teaching for transfer. The ultimate goal is to teach individuals how to be independent, so that metaphorically, the trapped fly is able to systematically solve how to escape the window.

So Clifford began to explore how to teach for transfer—how to teach individuals to use knowledge to make their own decisions and be independent—and it began early on, when he was teaching studio trumpet and applied brass at Florida State University.

> And I tell a story on a regular basis of watching doctoral students cry when they leave with a doctorate, saying, "Can I come back and take a private lesson?" And I think, "That is not what we ought to be doing." We ought to have people at the time they leave that are ready to fly. That we catapult them out of here into independent success. And if we're not doing that, then what we're doing is creating people that will be dependent on us.
>
> (Madsen, Clifford. Personal Interview. 12 May 2015)

Clifford began implementing transfer activities in his private trumpet studio teaching at FSU.

> When I was teaching trumpet from 1960 and applied brass, I said "Okay, my goal as a private instructor is to make myself dispensable as soon as possible." I said, "How am I going to do this?" Well, I'm going to teach you how to teach yourself. . . . And you ask students to do that (transfer) and they really do it well and they get good at it and then once it becomes habitual for them, it just opens up the whole world. So, that is on the way to becoming an independent person and being able to analyze what it is that I do that is meaningful. So, independence is a very important thing and that's what gets to the objectives determined by the value system. That's the student's value system and not mine.
>
> (Madsen, Clifford. Personal Interview. 12 May 2015)

Independence is the primary reason that Clifford teaches for transfer. Further, he wants his students to make their own decisions based on their own value system. Again, at the center of his philosophy is the empowerment of the individual. He earnestly desires to teach his students:

> that they be independent . . . that they analyze, criticize, choose alternatives . . . you know, the higher-order thinking that everybody just kind of discovered and, those are the first two objectives of every class I've ever had since I ever started to put syllabi together . . . to study something, analyze, criticize, choose alternatives, and act on a basis of some compelling value system that comes from you, one's own experience.
> (Madsen, Clifford. Personal Interview. 12 May 2015)

Because Clifford's philosophy includes empowering the individual, teaching the individual to choose, making decisions based on data, and transferring knowledge, it makes sense that, "From my point of view, empirical research and my philosophical position, and behavior modification are exactly the same" (Madsen, Clifford. Personal Interview. 19 June 2015). "*Experimental Research* and *Teaching/Discipline* and every other book that I've ever written is . . . trying to get people excited about the joy of learning, the joy of discovery" (Madsen, Clifford. Personal Interview. 29 June 2015).

Happiness

Everyone has the right to pursue happiness. Discovering what it is that makes one happy is at the crux of the ability to pursue happiness. Some people have trouble identifying their life course because they are dependent on the opinion of others, such that they are unable to choose for themselves. So Clifford tries to teach individuals to pursue what makes them happy—not what makes the teacher happy or the parents happy, but what makes the individual happy.

> It never mattered to me whether or not people who wanted to work with me, in little ways or big ways, were . . . I mean, they are band, or choral, or orchestra, or they want to do qualitative research or . . . that to me is just not very important. I mean it's not a question of converting people to the correct methodology or whatever. It's just seeing people get really excited and become really happy with what they're doing on a day-to-day basis that makes them happy and makes other people happy. So, that's what I would hope, that success is measured, for the most part, by the individual who is living the life.
> (Madsen, Clifford. Personal Interview. 29 June 2015)

The idea that individuals decide for themselves recurred throughout our interviews with Clifford and the interviews with his family and former students. "That's one thing that my dad really embodied—living your personal truth. Doing what you want to do and then you can share that with others" (Madsen, Katia. Personal Interview. 15 April 2016). In his classes, he frequently reminds students, "Don't let my biases be your biases," and he regularly encourages students to choose for themselves.

> Well, I am pleased when people are pleased with themselves. And if they're doing things and it makes them happy, if they get excited about research and they're curious and they just can't wait to find the results of a study or something then, yay! But people who are doing something that is negative, just waiting to get a little gleam of happiness from time to time. . . . It doesn't make much sense, because time is the only thing we have.
>
> (Madsen, Clifford. Personal Interview. 29 June 2015)

Time Is Life

Time—and more specifically, the perception of the passage of time—has preoccupied Clifford Madsen for many years. In fact, he even wrote an unpublished book that contemplates the construct of time and is entitled *Life's Time*. Below is an excerpt from the preface to that book.

> The present work regards time, not in the speculative, scientific, or occult sense, but rather in an everyday sense. It represents a "labor of love" that has preoccupied the author for many years. Indeed, the first draft of this manuscript was completed in 1973. Across these years (and many revised manuscript drafts) the major issue remains—life is time. Our lives, for the most part, exist in what might be called common, everyday temporal sequences—not necessarily limited to scientific boundaries nor even enhanced by speculation concerning aspects outside of commonplace time. It would seem that most people live within the temporal sequence of seconds, minutes, hours, days, and years. Indeed, within one's lifetime commonplace aspects of time prevail. Therefore, the present work seeks to investigate commonplace aspects of time and more importantly, to understand how structures within time can be changed to increase the sum total of life's positive experiences. This will not delight those who are looking for instant answers or a rationalization for boredom. It speaks to those who view life and its control as an ongoing, long-term process.[10]

How one uses time is of profound importance. In fact, one of the activities in *Teaching/Discipline* is to record a weekly time log. An interesting exercise is to compare one's values to how one actually uses time. If one's use of time is inconsistent with one's own values, then it warrants some reflection and possible reevaluation of either how time is spent, or the value system which one espouses.[11] In other words, if one is spending the majority of one's time doing something that one despises, why continue on that course? How one chooses to spend time should be congruent with one's values and priorities. On the other hand, Clifford also stresses the importance of understanding the difference between frequency and magnitude. The quantification of time is dependent on one's perspective, and certainly on the magnitude of a given event, which differs from frequency in terms of the intensity or impact that the event has on the individual.

> Frequency doesn't make nearly as much difference as magnitude. And I can remember as a college professor, I would sit here and talk to somebody for an hour and we would talk about any number of subjects or whatever but when they went out and talked about that with their friends they would say, "Well, you know, he spent a whole hour with me!" And if I were the person that they were talking to I would say, "Well what did you talk about?" And then they would likely say, "Well, you know, stuff, but a whole hour!" That's frequency. And one of the really selfish things that I do is to limit my social interaction with people that can't tell the difference between frequency and magnitude and they desperately need more frequency but what they never really developed is the capacity for magnitude.
>
> (Madsen, Clifford. Personal Interview. 26 June 2015)

An event of high magnitude is one that stays with an individual over time. We can all remember moments in our lives that were either high positive or high negative and, because of the intensity of the events, we do not forget them. Because the magnitude of an event is more important than the frequency, being truly "on task" is of utmost importance to Clifford. Focusing one's attention on a given task or individual increases the quality, intensity, or magnitude of the experience. This focus is in comparison to simply spending large quantities of time together, but without true interaction or engagement. He references this as "being alone together."

> [I]f I am talking to you and listening to you, my entire, everything in my mind is focused on you. It's focused. And a lot of people that have never learned to do that, or especially to value that (level of focus)—can't stand it. I don't know why, it's just . . . and they even use the word, "It's too intense." Well, how can it be too intense? Music can't be too intense. The most beautiful music in the world, to me, the very ending

> of Carlisle Floyd's *Of Mice and Men*. . . . Where most music ends with the loudest you can possibly get, that one ends, if I remember correctly, Lenny and the little dead mouse and it just fades into nothingness. And the best players that I know, they end the note while it's still in tune, in pitch and . . . and the entire audience doesn't really know when the pitch ended and the silence took over.
>
> (Madsen, Clifford. Personal Interview. 26 June 2015)

Because "everything relates to everything," one can see how empowerment, choosing, making choices based on data, deciding how to spend one's time, and pursuing what makes one happy are all, in a way, the same thing. Each of these values relates to the other, and can all be viewed through the lens of teaching independence by teaching individuals to transfer. Once these ideas are seen as related and inextricably linked, then it is easier to understand the philosophy, teaching, and life's work of Clifford Madsen.

Notes

1. Durant, Will. *The Story of Philosophy: The Lives and Opinions of the Great Philosophers of the Western World*. 2nd ed. New York: Simon and Schuster, 1961.
2. Madsen, Clifford K., and Charles H. Madsen, Jr. *Teaching/Discipline: A Positive Approach for Educational Development*. 5th ed. Raleigh, NC: Contemporary Publishing Company of Raleigh, 2016. P. 27.
3. Madsen, Clifford K. "Diversity in Thinking." Florida State Music Educators Association State Conference, 14 January 2016, Tampa Convention Center, Tampa, FL. Keynote Address.
4. Bennett, Barbara. *Oral Memoirs of Clifford K. Madsen*. Institute for Oral History. Baylor University, 2000. P. 2.
5. Madsen, Clifford K. Excerpt from "Who Claps for You?" Class Lecture, 12 June 2015, Florida State University.
6. Ullmann, Leonard P., and Leonard Krasner, Eds. *Case Studies in Behavior Modification*. New York: Holt, Rinehart and Winston, 1965.
7. Madsen, Clifford K., and Charles H. Madsen, Jr. *Teaching/Discipline: A Positive Approach for Educational Development*. 5th ed. Raleigh, NC: Contemporary Publishing Company of Raleigh, 2016.
8. Madsen, Clifford K., and Randall S. Moore. *Experimental Research in Music: Workbook in Design and Statistical Tests*. Rev. ed. Raleigh, NC: Contemporary Pub., 1978. Pp. 6–9.
9. Madsen, Clifford K., and Randall S. Moore. *Experimental Research in Music: Workbook in Design and Statistical Tests*. Rev. ed. Raleigh, NC: Contemporary Pub., 1978. P. 5.
10. Madsen, Clifford K. *Life's Time*. Unpublished manuscript. Personal Library of Clifford Madsen. n.d. P. 4.
11. Madsen, Clifford K., and Charles H. Madsen, Jr. *Teaching/Discipline: A Positive Approach for Educational Development*. 5th ed. Raleigh, NC: Contemporary Publishing Company of Raleigh, 2016.

5 Empowering Others

Living life consistent with one's values is perhaps the most important and powerful transfer an individual can make. To understand Clifford Madsen's life and work, we must understand how he lived the philosophy that he espoused. How did his philosophical beliefs transfer into his life, teaching, and scholarship? In this chapter, we illuminate the ways in which Clifford empowered and spoke on behalf of others.

Empowerment/Individual Choice

> "Knowledge is power."

Clifford believes that knowledge increases independence, and thus empowers individuals to make their own choices. This belief can be observed in his syllabi, grading policy, attendance policy, in-class transfers, and test construction. In all of Clifford's class syllabi, his first two course objectives read: 1) to stimulate thinking concerning scientific methodology, relating to life and the music profession; and 2) to demonstrate the ability to logically analyze, criticize, and/or choose alternatives consistent with some value orientation.

The second objective specifically articulates his philosophy that individuals should make decisions consistent with their own values, rather than the values of others. His students will recognize the phrase, "Don't let my biases be yours." Encouraging students to make choices based on their own value system is constantly present in his teaching, scholarship, and service activities. Spanning both teaching and research, the first chapter of his book *Teaching/Discipline* includes a learning activity where the reader clearly differentiates between values and techniques.[1] The values that we teach our students, children, and loved ones are those chosen by the *individual*. This consistent practice empowers Clifford's students to choose their own values carefully, as the choices we make in life are based on our values.

Upon reflection, one might ask how a grading policy can empower individuals. Clifford includes "extra evidence" as a component in all of his courses for students who wish to earn an A grade. If all class assignments are completed, the student automatically earns a B. However, if extra evidence is completed satisfactorily, the grade is raised to an A. Extra evidence is one way that Clifford encourages creativity and independence in his students. Students decide for themselves to earn a grade of B or A through choosing an additional project. He discussed this decision to incorporate extra evidence in his class in one of our interviews:

> The reason I did that (added extra evidence) was way back when Laura Dorow was here and that was the first . . . easily five years I was teaching. . . . And the whole thing was competency based, through an A. . . . And she said, "Well, I don't want an A if everybody can get an A." Okay . . . so now, you've got to do something extra. "Well, what?" I'm not going to tell you. That's why it is extra evidence. You decide what to do. If I decide what it is, then it is just another assignment.
>
> (Madsen, Clifford. Personal Interview. 19 June 2015)

Another example of empowering student choice is illustrated through Clifford's attendance policy. He makes no differentiation between excused and unexcused absences. He simply decides at what point the integrity of his class will be compromised, and makes that timeframe the maximum number of allowable absences. Rather than having students email him to receive permission to miss class, he allows them to decide for themselves whether they will be absent because of illness, a family emergency, or simply because they need some time for a mental health break. There is no penalty and no reason for requesting approval, because the student chooses how to use the allotted absences. The notion of an excused absence is problematic for Clifford because it employs two people's value systems simultaneously: the teacher's and the student's. First, teachers' and students' value systems regarding student time use frequently conflict. Giving approval for a student to miss a class sends mixed signals regarding the importance of attending class, yet there may be many reasons that require a student to miss class. Missing class is the choice of the student, thus removing the need for the teacher to approve of an absence. He explains this attendance policy further:

> An excused absence is an oxymoron. I mean, if somebody were to just take that to an extreme. . . . It is the ability to think through a concept. So, excused from what and for how long? "Well, I was sick . . . excused from this." . . . "Well, how much excused from this? How about we just say excused from half the class? How about excused from the entire

> class? How about excused for a year? How about being excused for the entire time? The college degree? How about being excused from life?" *(chuckling)* And they get all angry. . . . "Well, that's not what I mean. You know what I mean." I know exactly what they think they mean. But they don't understand what they are saying. "Well, can't you be here and not be here at the same time?" And, of course, what they are really saying is, "Is my grade going to suffer?" And when I say, with or without excuse or sickness or anything else, I mean it. And it is at that point that I have already predetermined where the integrity of the course is diminished. Additionally, the whole idea that we spend an hour of people's time or 50 minutes or an hour and a half of people's time. . . . The student says, "Well, did I miss anything important?" I say, "Don't you understand what an insult that is?" No, we were here for an hour and 20 minutes and it didn't matter if we were here or we talked about anything. . . .*(laughing and chuckling)* "Well, you know what I mean." "No, I don't know what you mean. What do you mean?"
>
> (Madsen, Clifford. Personal Interview. 19 June 2015)

Daily written transfers are a trademark of the first 5 minutes of every class. These transfers offer students the opportunity to choose their own focus of learning as it relates to their value system, placing the learner at the center of instruction. Clifford reads these transfers religiously after each class and incorporates the students' ideas, understandings, misconceptions, or experiences into subsequent classes. His students regularly reflect that they feel as if "he is speaking directly to me" during class. Even Clifford's tests offer the opportunity for personal choice, as students demonstrate their understanding of content presented in class. Students are given permission to change the questions on Clifford's tests if they want to convey their understanding of a topic or related concept in a different way.

> They say there is no such thing as a wrong answer, just the wrong question. And if you think about that, it is probably more true than not. So, if somebody, especially on a multiple-choice or . . . because most people have been conditioned all of their lives to these subtle little gotchas. . . . They include footnotes in the test. You are not going to find it in the regular test, you are going to find it in the notes at the end in the back. Gotcha! And . . . I don't want to do that.
>
> (Madsen, Clifford. Personal Interview. 19 June 2015)

When one reflects deeply on this practice, a thoughtful teacher will realize that test construction, grading policies, and attendance policies all employ the value system of the teacher. By empowering students to make choices regarding attendance, transfers, grading, and testing, Clifford places students at the center of instruction, optimizing their independence and prioritizing their personal educational journey.

Empowerment Through Research and Creative Activity

Clifford's research and creative activity also focuses on empowering others through the creation of new instructional materials designed to support student learning, or through collaborations with others that provide mentorship as they enter the college teaching profession. Clifford's doctoral students each complete one research project of their choice in collaboration with him during their degree. He frequently asks his students, "Well, what is your project going to be?" Jayne Standley recalled that he not only asked this question during her degree, but following her graduation, to encourage her consistent and future productivity:

> Clifford would say: "What are you doing this coming AMTA conference, and what's the article? I need the title today." . . .*(laughing)* And, I'm thinking about health services for the State of Florida and he's calling in May saying, "What's the title of the presentation you are doing in November?" And I said, "What?" And I said, "Well, Cliff, I'll call you and give me an hour." "No." Because, he won't let you put it off. It's not that he needs it that minute. He needs you to make a decision and a commitment. Then you learn, "Gosh, if I have to make up a title and then do something I didn't want to do, I think I'll think about it ahead of time and decide on what I'm going to give him" *(laughing throughout)*.
>
> (Standley, Jayne. Personal Interview. 29 June 2015)

Of his 12 published texts, all were written to assist others in their personal learning, and many were collaborations with his doctoral students. The texts included here are those he coauthored with students. His first book, *Experimental Research in Music*,[2] was written and published by Prentice-Hall in 1969, shortly after Clifford began teaching the Psychology of Music course.

> [A]nd the reason I did that is because when I started to teach the Psych of Music classes, the textbook at the time had this cover of this guy with a big magnifying glass in front of his face. You could see that it was obviously a book for sixth grade or fifth grade. And I thought, "There ought to be something that is more sophisticated without getting into really sophisticated research designs." And so, out of necessity . . . most everything I've done is because there was no textbook for it.
>
> (Madsen, Clifford. Personal Interview. 1 July 2015)

The workbook written to accompany the text, published in 1978, was a series of statistics modules designed to assist students in acquiring the necessary statistical skills to become effective researchers. Clifford's doctoral students were currently taking statistics classes, and it was they who created the individual programs within the workbook. Randall Moore designed a number of the program learning modules in the workbook, and became a coauthor of the book.[3] He shared the following in an interview:

> This was another example of his loving mentorship, that he would care enough to coauthor and supervise us because he knew that this would professionally put us on the map, and that we needed it for survival. Because, you know, one of the continual topics of group discussion was survival. Get a job is number one; the second is, how do you survive the job? That's even more difficult (*laughs*). So just giving us a boost, you know? Even when I was there, a bunch of us together under Cliff's mentorship, we'd have at least one group research project we would do every year, and we'd write it up and it'd be published! So, I got the *Experimental Research* book and two research articles with Cliff and some other folks there published.
>
> (Moore, Randall. Personal Interview. 26 April 2016)

Another project published by Clifford and his very first graduate student, Douglas Greer, was *Research in Music Behavior: Modifying Music Behavior in the Classroom*.[4] This text, published by Teachers College Press in 1975, was a compilation of behavior studies conducted by graduate students of both Douglas and Clifford. Douglas was on the faculty at Teachers College:

> We were doing programmatic research, and no one was doing any programmatic research then in music. I had a connection with Teachers College Press, the press that published it. In fact, that I was here helped some in getting it published. And so, it was just a natural outcome of our collaboration, because we were collaborating back and forth.
>
> (Greer, Douglas. Personal Interview. 2 June 2016)

Clifford coauthored *Contemporary Music Education*[5] with Terry Kuhn, another doctoral student. While teaching at FSU, Clifford volunteered to teach the course Music for the Elementary Teacher. He began looking for a methodology that he thought would best suit that course, and found many resources on how to present various topics, but nothing that really got to the most poignant or important questions that he felt preservice teachers should consider.

> Because, why should you teach? You know the old preacher. The preacher has two tasks, to comfort the afflicted and afflict the comfortable. But I was definitely trying to afflict the comfortable and get them to think about all the incongruities in their present life and try and get them to think realistically about what it meant to be a teacher, very much like the programs with parenting where they actually take a young teenage girl and have her carry around a doll 24/7 just to see what it is to have somebody needing care 24/7. . . . But, I was just trying to ask questions to get people to think about what they were going to do.
>
> (Madsen, Clifford. Personal Interview. 1 July 2015)

Terry was assisting Clifford with that course, and *Contemporary Music Education* became the project that he selected as his collaboration. Terry recalled:

> Cliff always liked to publish something with each student that he directed. His belief was that you should leave with some kind of publication record. So, he just asked me straight out one day . . . "What would you like to do with me in your third year?" I said that I would like to take his lectures in the *Music for Elementary Teachers* course and capture them into book form. And, he kind of looked at me. I mean, it wasn't research as experimental research goes but I had always been fascinated with what he did in that class. And it was more "Cliff the philosopher," not "Cliff the statistician" or "Cliff the researcher," but Cliff thinking about life and what was important. And I thought, "That's what I want." So, I taped and transcribed every one of those lectures for a whole semester and I typed them out. Now, that's the first half of the book. That's the good half of the book. That's Cliff's half.
>
> (Kuhn, Terry. Personal Interview. 26 February 2016)

Competency-Based Music Education was first published in 1980 and coauthored by Clifford and Cornelia Yarbrough,[6] another doctoral student. At the time, Cornelia was working with Robert Braunagel (see Chapter 3). Braunagel had created a manual that he gave to student teachers to help prepare them for work in the public schools. Using the manual as a model, Cornelia created a systematic approach for competency-based music education, "because all of us here at FSU were on that path right from the very beginning. And so, that was the impetus and the ideology, if you will, of that book. That was something that Cornelia did with me and for me" (Madsen, Clifford. Personal Interview. 29 June 2015).

Applications of Research in Music Behavior[7] was a compilation of research studies edited by Clifford and former doctoral student Carol

Prickett. Clifford had been invited as an endowed chair professor for a one-month residency at the University of Alabama, Carol's university.

> This was one of those career boosts; when he was invited to be endowed chair professor for a month in residence in January of 1985. He had decided that we would publish a series of papers as this applications book—which was a sequel to the research book that he had done with Doug Greer back in the '70s, and he wanted to do another edition of a book like that. He had this stature in the profession and the University of Alabama Press had agreed that they would publish this, but this would be my chance to be the editor and to get some experience doing that. Again, I'm a comma and grammar person; I always said, "He did substance and I did form." So, we had people submit their papers, and then we had to figure out how to group them, how to introduce them; these were experienced publishers but they still . . . boy did I know the APA manual by the time we finished that! But it was such a pleasure to go through these papers or to see how they sort of broke into categories or common interests, and then to try to thread them together and then we edited them. Jane Cassidy and another person in Tallahassee went over proofs with me.
>
> (Prickett, Carol. Personal Interview. 28 April 2016)

Across his career, Clifford continued the practice of coauthoring various manuscripts with his graduate students. The aforementioned projects constitute the major texts that were collaborations with students. Numerous research studies were also supervised by Clifford throughout his college teaching career. When asked about research collaborations, Clifford shared:

> For the most part, the collaboration comes for two reasons. One, if there are people whom I can help to catapult into the field, then I think it's my responsibility to help them as much as I can. And, getting them involved in research, letting them do some presentations, and coauthor, or whatever. And then, if I continue to work with those people . . . some I do and most I don't, it's only because their specific interests are more aligned to what my interests are at that particular point in time.
>
> (Madsen, Clifford. Personal Interview. 1 July 2015)

Clifford has been chairing the Music Education/Therapy/Contemporary Media department at FSU for over 40 years. In that role, one of the first decisions he made was to eliminate meetings to protect the faculty's time, because he believes that meetings inhibit individual choice regarding time use, thus limiting productivity. He spoke of the issue of meetings in his Senior Researcher Award address at MENC:

> It is often said that a heavy teaching assignment reduces research productivity. This is often the case, but it seems to me that the primary enemy is not teaching but unnecessary meetings. Disregard for faculty time has no parallel when it comes to scheduling meetings. While faculty participation in the running of a university is both important and necessary, it seems that quality time is far more important than total time, and every attempt should be made to limit meetings. As one might suspect, I have collected data on this aspect as well as other issues dealing with use of time, and I would suggest that a great deal of research could be accomplished during the time devoted to committee meetings.[8]

Along with increased autonomy in regard to time, he gave faculty ownership over the courses they taught. One could choose to teach whatever courses one wished, as long as they did not encroach on another person's area. Most importantly, he supported the development of a tenure/annual review process that included a comprehensive view of scholarship. Faculty were able to contribute in a variety of ways to their research agenda that included performing, conducting, researching, and presenting.

Speaking on Behalf of Others

> "I am an old, rich, white, heterosexual male. I advocate for everything I am not: poor, LGBTQ, women, children, and all minorities."

Clifford is a strong and active advocate for marginalized populations. He spends considerable time and financial resources seeking to enfranchise the disenfranchised. Moreover, in his teaching, he seeks to increase students' awareness of inequity. As part of his College Teaching in Music class, for example, Clifford has all of his students do individual presentations, bringing attention to important issues in higher education. In preparation for these presentations, he will often bring in copies of the latest issues of the periodical *Chronicle of Higher Education* and ask his students whether they would like to consider the featured article. Very intentionally, he will ask that students of color NOT choose racism as their topic, and that gay students NOT choose homophobia as their topic. Instead, he asks that someone who does not represent those populations consider the topic, in the hope that they will learn something about an experience that is foreign to their own, and empathize with and later advocate for those populations. Nicole Robinson, an

African-American woman and former student in that class, recently wrote about this experience:

> There was a class assignment where we had to debate various topics in his College Teaching course. One of the topics was "Racism in Higher Education." Being the only Black in the class, I assumed that "Racism in Higher Education" would automatically be assigned to me. Why, of course! Right?! As soon as I saw the list of topics, I was already framing stories of how I had experienced racism throughout my life, one being when in (undergraduate) college, my friend and I went to sublease an apartment during the summer and although everything had been settled on the phone, when we knocked on the door to visit the landlord's house to pay the deposit, she opened the door and said "We don't have an apartment available." We were confused, checked the address with her and she said "Yes, this is the correct address, but we don't have a unit available."
>
> As we walked away, we noticed a pathway that led to the back where there was an apartment attached to the home. We knocked and the younger white gentleman said, "Yes, you're in the correct place." He had posted the ad to sublease his unit because he was going home for the summer. It was a cool conversation—he was at Duke, we were at NCCU. He shared rules, processes, arranged the sublease, and we were set. We were so excited! The next day, he called and said he was not allowed to sublease to us. When we asked why; he said the landlord said she would not rent to blacks (yes! in the mid-'90s). He was just as shocked as we were and really felt bad he had to deliver this news.
>
> Now, back to Clifford K. Madsen. As you can imagine, I just KNEW he was going to assign "Racism in Higher Education" to me. I mean . . . who else could it be, but me?? I could immediately imagine in my mind's eye how I would use the housing story to frame my presentation. BUT, Dr. Madsen assigned that topic to one of my white colleagues. What???? How could he?? I was so upset. I went straight to his office afterward and said "How can you give the topic of racism to HIM?? How can HE speak about racism when he has never experienced racism?" That is when Dr. Madsen planted one of the most golden nuggets of wisdom in me.
>
> He said, "Nicole-love, you have to learn, those with power must speak for those without power. So, men have to speak for women, white people have to speak up for people of color, heterosexuals have to speak for those in the LGBTQ community, etc." I have to admit, I did not fully understand what he was teaching me at the time, but it would undergird my teaching, research, and service today.

> I will always remember the day when my white colleague stood up (I still had a slight attitude, mind you:)) and started his presentation with deep pregnant pauses. "I. NEVER. KNEW. I. NEVER. KNEW of the appalling and shocking things I learned about racism in higher education. . . ." The room was silenced as we all sat on the edge of our seats and began traveling down this journey with my colleague as he shared his discoveries about "Racism in Higher Education." Afterward, Dr. Madsen asked me . . . "Now, do you understand? Those with the power should speak for those without power."[9]

Racism is an issue that Clifford has fought for many years, and he has spent a long time thinking about how he might use his position of privilege to stand up for others, even when it was potentially threatening to his employment. Integration was at its height during the first years of Clifford's teaching at FSU (early 1960s) as a full-time instructor, and Clifford was active in doing what he thought was right within the community and city. He was responsible for developing the first integrated symposium between the sister institution in Tallahassee, the Florida Agricultural and Mechanical University (FAMU), a historically black college, and FSU. The symposium was called "Decreasing Racial Tension," and an equal number of white and black participants met on the FAMU campus for several days and then at FSU. Because almost everything in Tallahassee was not integrated, arrangements had to be made to house the black participants arriving from outside cities. After this lodging was accomplished, the symposium went on for several days without any interference from anyone.

During that same time, Clifford was participating in a boycott of a restaurant across the street from the School of Music, The Mecca, because they refused to serve students of color. Shortly thereafter, Dean Karl Kuersteiner called Clifford into his office to discuss a logistics issue related to storage of old instruments. During this pleasant exchange, Clifford mentioned to Kuersteiner his idea of establishing a new Center for Music Research within the School of Music. Kuersteiner became engaged and said, "Well, this sounds like a very good idea; let's continue our discussion over lunch." Clifford was absolutely delighted. He had never been invited to the Dean's office, let alone to discuss anything of substance. Clifford was extremely excited about having lunch with him. Then the Dean said, "Well, we will eat across the street where those hoodlums are picketing."

Clifford remembers his stomach tightening and saw his entire career at FSU flash before his eyes. After what seemed like a thousand years, Clifford said, "Well, I guess we will not have lunch, sir—I'm one of those hoodlums." He quickly left the Dean's office and that evening told his wife,

Mary, "Well, honey, pack your bags, because my life is over at FSU." Without tenure, he just assumed his career had ended in Tallahassee.

However, the subsequent summer Clifford was hired to assist with the Summer Music Camps. Kuersteiner had expanded the camps to bring in revenue so that every faculty wanting employment during the summer could be hired with the camp funds. The camps were very large. Along with bands and choruses, there were at least six sections of baton twirling for high school students, along with drum major leadership sessions, etc. All of the campers, however—then, as now—had to take other classes in music theory and history. Graduate students, whose pay was minuscule compared to faculty, taught almost all of the camps. Clifford's pay as a graduate assistant was also very low, and he was hired to teach music theory at the camp. During one of the classes he was teaching, an older woman approached Clifford at the classroom door and asked if she could observe the class. Clifford said, "Sure, take a seat." He assumed that she was the mother of one of the young girls in the class. After the class, she said nothing and excused herself.

Years later, Clifford met the Dean of Faculties, Larry Chalmers. Clifford knew that Chalmers had been concerned with Dean Kuersteiner's outspoken antagonism against persons of color. Once during a meeting, Kuersteiner said repeatedly that he did not want any interactions with FAMU. Clifford remembers that during one meeting, when someone suggested working with the music program at FAMU, Kuersteiner said, "We do not want our white girls canoeing down the river with those colored boys." This statement always disturbed Clifford, as well as many others, yet everyone knew about the Dean's strong opinions about persons of color.

Dean of Faculties Chalmers abhorred Kuersteiner's sentiments, and as his superior, initiated the process of forcing Kuersteiner to retire. Kuersteiner, however, did not want to retire, and stated it repeatedly. One technique Chalmers had devised was to expose what he considered the "sham" of young high school girls coming to Tallahassee to twirl batons all day long. Kuersteiner refused to retire, and after several contentious months in office, literally had to be physically removed from his office. A few years later, when Clifford happened to be seated next to Dr. Chalmers, Chalmers told him that the person who had observed Clifford's summer music theory camp class was his administrative assistant, who previously had been a music education undergraduate. She just went into the first Summer Music Camp class she encountered. She reported back to Chalmers that Clifford's class was some of the best music teaching she had ever seen. As Clifford did not know Chalmers, he always assumed that Chalmers was the person responsible for Clifford keeping his job after the ill-fated lunch invitation. Clifford never heard about it again. The Center for Music Research was established several years after Kuersteiner's retirement. Additionally, Clifford was instrumental in hiring Amy Brown, who was the first person of color to join the School of Music faculty. Since that time, the diversity of the faculty has continued to increase.

Clifford's sensitivity to inclusion extended to language use in one of his textbooks, *Competency-Based Music Education*, coauthored with Cornelia Yarbrough.[10] Originally published in 1980, Clifford clarifies that in an effort to include everyone, there is not one he/she pronoun:

> at that time many of us were sensitized to the injustices of a male-dominated society and we still are, and we are not there yet. As everyone knows, right now in this day and age, we have a whole group of people that were not prepared to vote for Hillary Clinton for no other reason than they don't recognize this deep-seated prejudice against women. And, I think it's pretty obvious. It's obvious in the way people think, and write, and do. And as you know, that's one of my passions in life. I just wanted to make sure that if I could do anything about it, the girls in my family would see themselves as having the same possibilities as any boy would have. And that was important to me way back in the 1970s. As I say, we are not there yet.
>
> (Madsen, Clifford. Personal Interview. 1 July 2015)

Carol Prickett reflects on how inclusive Clifford is with women, considering them equals in the profession:

> And Cornelia—who is a strong personality—I know strong personalities (*laughs*)—but we have laughed and said no matter how hard we would push or argue with Cliff about something, and really, really be passionate about an argument, he never flinched from that. We were always treated as an equal. And I think if you see him with Mary, you understand that, and you see where that comes from and how it's grown, but that's a unique privilege in any profession and certainly in academia, and that's still true today.
>
> (Prickett, Carol. Personal Interview. 28 April 2016)

Because of Clifford's continued advocacy for the LGBTQ community, Louis Bergonzi, Conference Chair, invited Clifford to be a keynote speaker at the first national conference of the LGBT music community (Establishing Identity: LGBT Studies and Music Education) at the University of Illinois. Some highlights of his speech appear below:

> I want again to reiterate that it is incumbent upon us, those of us who are in power, to help others. I think we should try to be as good mentors as we can. I think those of us who hold a power advantage ought to make

sure that we mentor others in the long-term process of research and teaching, and that includes helping them with the fruits of academia, the coin of the realm in all of its forms including promotion and tenure.

I have benefited greatly from the shared experiences of others and realized a long time ago that there are many things we as college professors can do to increase awareness and acceptance of LGBTQ issues. One very important aspect is to strive to include all allies who attempt to feel the pain of LGBTQ oppression and rectify historical injustices. Please include all of us who know that this should be a non-issue but realize that everyone has both the responsibility and needs to develop the courage to "stand up and be counted."

Personally, I have learned to take the natural opportunities that present themselves to talk about these issues in class—especially when unique opportunities present themselves. One of my favorite male transgender students showed up one day in a skirt. I thought it absolutely delightful that they felt comfortable doing it. When one class member said something derogatory about choosing to be gay under his breath, I took the opportunity to discuss it in class and asked that student "When did you decide to be straight?"

It seems to me the most parsimonious explanation for sexual preference is that it is normally distributed—that it approximates a stochastic distribution. If one thinks of both male and female persons along a "normal curve" (no pun intended), then it is apparent that most folks form the middle of the distribution and are heterosexual—more or less. As one contemplates the slopes from the middle then on one side there would be males who relate to each other; on the other side we would have females that relate to each other. There would also be approximately 14–15% on each side "leaning" toward complete same-sex identification with still fewer who would constitute the third standard deviation (again no pun intended) on each side representing *only* same-sex propensities. This explanation does not argue with "choice versus DNA," it just describes the state of an entire group of people's orientation.

Lastly, I have a personal request to make to all the people here. Please continue to do research about all the myriad issues concerning the LGBTQ community. I think research activities that do this will be extremely useful in dissemination, especially qualitative research, because the narrative stories that it tells I think will touch other people's hearts, minds, and souls, in a very substantive manner, as do excellent plays and movies.[11]

As is typical of a prolific researcher in the field, Clifford is often asked to write letters of support for tenure and promotion for faculty in music education. When asked how he chooses which to write, given the large number of requests, he explains that "It's easy, I do all of the people who have been traditionally discriminated against: 1) women, 2) persons of color, 3) LGBTQ persons—if out and I know who they are, and 4) general music teachers. Then I do the others for which I have time" (Madsen, Clifford. Personal Interview. 19 June 2015).

His colleague at FSU, Amy Brown, nominated Clifford for the Dr. Martin Luther King, Jr. service award in 1997. In her letter of support,[12] Amy writes: "'What are you doing for others?' Martin Luther King Jr. spent and literally lost his life answering this question. Cliff practices the grace and love in order to serve and enhance the lives of others." Recounting examples wherein Clifford embodies the principles of Martin Luther King, Jr., she continues:

> Concerning human interdependence, former students often quote Madsen's contention that the privileged must take care of the underprivileged, the rich the poor, the straight the gay, the healthy the ill, and the smart the not too smart. Concerning racism, his students learn that as Martin Luther King Jr. said, all racism is evil and black racism is just as evil as white racism, a degrading unacceptable condition. . . . Madsen's civil rights activities during his traditionally busy doctoral student days at FSU are legendary. He found time to participate in peaceful demonstrations against the coffee shop across the street from the School of Music where black students were refused service. He found places in Tallahassee where black and white music students could play jazz together since the School of Music denied them access. And he also took the leadership in organizing and integrating a FAMU chapter of the formerly exclusively white national college music fraternity, Phi Mu Alpha. These activities are all in keeping with Dr. Martin Luther King Jr.'s belief that blacks and whites could only come to understand each other through contact. . . . Clifford Madsen spends his life opening pathways for others.

Clifford spent many years of his life committed to service, at FSU and nationally/internationally, serving the profession of music education and music therapy. He has won numerous awards for his service, including 51 years on the Faculty Senate and 39 years on the Faculty Senate Steering Committee. FSU honored him with a citation in 2015. Ever the observer, he always took notes at these meetings, looking for opportunities to lead and serve:

> This is why, and I've said this before in other places, this is why I always take notes. I'm the worst note-taker. My penmanship is awful.

> But, in a meeting people always look to the woman in the group or whatever . . . to get the coffee or tea. For 30 or 40 years on the Senate Steering Committee, I made sure that I was the one who made the coffee, served the coffee, and cleaned up. And, it's not that big of a deal. But it sends more than a subtle message to people that it's okay. . . . There is no such thing as women's work and men's work. There is people work. I grew up in a very liberated house. I don't think my mother did very much work at all because she taught her children how to clean and cook and take care of themselves.
>
> (Madsen, Clifford. Personal Interview. 1 July 2015)

Clifford is a lifetime member of the National Association for the Advancement of Colored People and the Council for Exceptional Education of Children. He works very deliberately to bring issues of racism, sexism, homophobia, and all forms of discrimination to the forefront of his discussions in and outside of class with his students.

Notes

1. Madsen, Clifford K., and Charles H. Madsen, Jr. *Teaching/Discipline: A Positive Approach for Educational Development.* 5th ed. Raleigh, NC: Contemporary Publishing Company of Raleigh, 2016. P. 27.
2. Madsen, Clifford K., and Charles H. Madsen Jr. *Experimental Research in Music.* Englewood Cliffs, NJ: Prentice-Hall, 1970.
3. Madsen, Clifford K., and Randall S. Moore. *Experimental Research in Music: Workbook in Design and Statistical Tests.* Rev. ed. Raleigh, NC: Contemporary Pub., 1978.
4. Madsen, Clifford K., et al. *Research in Music Behavior: Modifying Music Behavior in the Classroom.* New York: Teachers College Press, 1975.
5. Madsen, Clifford K., and Terry Lee Kuhn. *Contemporary Music Education.* Northbrook, IL: AHM Pub. Corp., 1978.
6. Madsen, Clifford K., and Cornelia Yarbrough. *Competency-Based Music Education.* Englewood Cliffs, NJ: Prentice-Hall, 1980.
7. Madsen, Clifford K., and Carol A. Prickett, Eds. *Applications of Research in Music Behavior.* Tuscaloosa, AL: University of Alabama Press, 1987.
8. Madsen, Clifford K. "Senior Researcher Award Acceptance Address." *Journal of Research in Music Education*, vol. 36, no. 3, 1988. P. 134.
9. Robinson, Nicole. "Facebook Post About Dr. Clifford Madsen's Mentorship." Facebook, 26 March 2018. www.facebook.com/nicole.r.robinson.1/posts/10157799412879852. Accessed 11 December 2018.
10. Madsen, Clifford K., and Cornelia Yarbrough. *Competency-Based Music Education.* Englewood Cliffs, NJ: Prentice-Hall, 1980.
11. Madsen, Clifford. "LGBT Conference Summary." *Establishing Identity: Lesbian, Gay, Bisexual and Transgender Studies and Music Education*, May 2010, University of Illinois, Urbana, IL. Keynote Address.
12. Brown, Amy. Letter to the Martin Luther King, Jr. Distinguished Service Award Committee. 13 January 1997. Florida State University, Tallahassee, FL.

6 A (Positive) Behavioral Approach

"Behavior is true."

Clifford is perhaps best known for his positive behavioral approach, which manifests in his teaching, research, and service. While many people associate behaviorism with manipulation of rats and other controversial/unethical treatment of others, Clifford would argue that many of these people are confusing values with techniques. Values are ideas that can be taught, while techniques constitute the reinforcements and consequences for specific behaviors.[1] A behavioral approach is neither inherently good or bad, because it is up to individuals to choose the values they will teach and the behavioral techniques they will use. Humans can use behavioral principles to effect positive or negative change. Certainly, a negative approach with strong consequences can be very effective in the short term (e.g., if someone holds a gun to someone's head, that person will likely immediately engage in the requested behavior) and is one example of a behavioral approach; however, Clifford Madsen advocates for a positive behavioral approach, guided by a value system that prioritizes positive outcomes.

The textbook *Teaching/Discipline*, coauthored with his brother Charles H. Madsen, Jr., embodies Clifford's beliefs about teaching, which are inextricably linked with discipline. He discussed drafting the first edition of the book and the thinking behind the title:

> It's a strange title, *Teaching/Discipline*. Charley and I worked with that title for a long time because we wanted the book to address discipline, but we wanted the book to address discipline in classroom management from a positive rather than a punitive basis. You see, when most people think of disciplining, they think of disciplining inappropriate social behavior, and yet we wanted to make a strong statement that was also consistent with the research literature, that teachers are the

> most powerful sources of reinforcement in classrooms. And if they will understand the power of their position, as it were, and understand how to interact with youngsters and oldsters, too, in basically a positive and encouraging but contingent way, that's a much better thing to do than to do nothing and then start to punish misbehavior and spend all their day or most of their day saying, "Be quiet. Sit down. Don't do that again," and having so-called discipline problems. So, the title of the book was purposely done to try to get people to understand that there is a need for structure, there is a need for some kind of schedule, a need for rules, which doesn't mean that society ought not to be in the process of establishing those rules. We encourage teachers with students of all ages to enlist the students in making up the rules and expectations and whatever, and to keep the rules simple, and to phrase the rules positively. Instead of saying, "Don't talk," say, "We interact quietly." And then to catch youngsters being good. That's a phrase that's fairly common nowadays. That's a phrase that was coined by Charley way back when. . . . So, the title of that book was basically designed to address the issue of teaching classroom teachers.[2]

When asked of his initial interest in behavioral principles, he commented:

> I have experienced only two academic epiphanies in my lifetime. The first was toward the end of the third grade, when I realized for the very first time I was actually reading. That is, not just looking at separate and small groups of words while not making a lot of sense out of it, but really going to a different place beyond the words. The second time was when I actually stopped to think about a basic concept I was reading about [John Stuart Mill's *Utilitarianism*],[3] "humans seek pleasure and avoid pain." That concept had always been there, as it is for most people. However, I remember stopping whatever I was doing at the time and making sundry connections about that basic idea. I started with what I had at that time garnered from reading philosophy, and quickly moved through my entire life's experiences all the time relating these to that basic concept. Of course, it became vividly obvious and just made sense. After a time, I started to wonder why anyone would argue with this basic premise. This is what we do all of the time—we avoid pain and seek pleasure.
>
> (Madsen, Clifford. Personal Interview. 20 September 2018)

This basic principle, that humans avoid pain and seek pleasure, is fundamental to a behavioral approach. The *Teaching/Discipline* book includes a learning activity that asks the reader to translate commonly used words that represent ideas concerning social behavior into specific overt, demonstrable behaviors. Therefore, an idea (value) such as "honesty" can be defined as "returns materials" and "verbalizes facts." Both are observable behaviors that can be measured. Readers are then encouraged to select techniques—positive ones—that can be used to reinforce these behaviors when observed.

The *Teaching/Discipline* text provides numerous examples of humans seeking pleasure and avoiding pain through clinical examples in the second section of the book. These examples utilize the pinpoint model, which provides a framework for conducting behavioral research. The model is structured in four steps. The first step is to Pinpoint explicitly a behavior that is to be increased or decreased. In the next step, Record, one specifies the behaviors across time intervals as the baseline. Consequate, a word they created, happens when contingencies are set up with some kind of reinforcement technique (approval, withholding of approval, disapproval, threat of disapproval, ignoring, etc.). Finally, at the Evaluate step, one takes data to determine whether the behavior has increased, decreased, or remained the same since the baseline step.

As an extension of the pinpoint model, one of the learning activities is a self-shaping project. Incorporating the pinpoint model, students choose an observable behavior that they wish to increase, decrease, or start/stop; record baseline data; select a consequate; and then record data to evaluate. The self-shaping project allows students to examine what is reinforcing and punishing for them (seek pleasure/avoid pain). If, for example, someone chooses to increase healthy eating behaviors, they might decide to reward themselves by doing something nice for themselves (manicure, pedicure, reading a book chapter, etc.) when they eat a vegetable at a meal; if they eat an unhealthy meal, they may choose to do a series of sit-ups that day. The goal is to learn about themselves while applying a behavioral approach.

Modeling

Clifford models a behavioral approach for his students through his teaching and productivity. In *Teaching/Discipline*, Clifford posits that "we control the environment that in turn controls us."[4] He elaborates on this idea when thinking about the way in which he prepares for his class:

> Well, first of all, I go in the night before and make sure that, if at all possible, I don't have one extra chair in the room. For any number of reasons, if you have 45 people in a class and you have 45 chairs then when you come in and everybody's in their chair, you don't even have to take roll that day because everybody's there. If you have an extra chair and you only have one, you can certainly account for that or two

> or three. But, to me, going into a room that has 50 chairs and you have 14 people in your class . . . it really is arranging the environment . . . controlling the environment that in turn controls you. And I go in the night before and move every chair, pick up stuff on the floor, make sure it's clean, make sure the chalkboard is clean, make sure there is some chalk there, make sure that all the media work . . . everything. And, that's really important to me. And it's not just kind of important, it's important enough so that every single night before my class the next day, I arrange everything.
>
> (Madsen, Clifford. Personal Interview. 12 May 2015)

Another way in which Clifford's behavioral philosophy is implemented regularly with his students is through his modeling of professionalism and productivity. It is remarkable how many of his doctoral students have learned to be productive scholars because they were expected to present regularly at conferences and publish their research. Clifford models behaviors of research productivity for others. When asked what advice he might provide to other researchers in music education, Clifford opines:

> The best single indicator of future behavior is past and present behavior, so that's why I think it's important, getting back to people who are going to identify themselves as researchers that we give them the catapults into the field and support those early years . . . it's inconceivable to me that a major professor could not do the research that they are asking a student to do. Like their job is to convene a committee. And, I have a problem with that as I'm sure you know.
>
> And you know that I use this analogy many times: If you want to learn to play the piano, you wouldn't sit around for 5 or 10 or 15 years, listening to great piano players, and being so critical that you could tell the little tiny nuances of each one compared to the other, but then you sit down at the piano and you can't play a C scale. Why it is that people think that you learn how to do research by being research critics? It's just anathema.
>
> I think it just starts with basic curiosity, tenacity that comes from a reinforcement schedule that we can actually teach and control to some degree. And then, taking joy by doing that along the way. And not being too upset by the rejections from people who are upset that we didn't write the research report like they think we should have written it, or, you know . . . all those kinds of things that get in the way. So, you have to have kind of a tough skin. I said in a speech I gave for Chris Johnson a couple of years ago that I've been turned down by every single journal in music and lots of others. When I said that,

> everybody laughed, and I wasn't sure why they laughed at the time. But my point was, that if one is going to give up after the first time that they don't get what they want, they are going to be a really unhappy camper.
>
> (Madsen, Clifford. Personal Interview. 1 July 2015)

Behavioral Research

Much of Clifford's research is behavioral. He coauthored the book *Research in Music Behavior*[5] with Douglas Greer and Charles H. Madsen, Jr., in an endeavor to present behavioral studies of research in music education and music therapy. There were not many models for behavioral research at that time. Clifford was the first music education researcher to use subject matter to reinforce other subject matter. In his 1979 study, "The Effect of Music Subject Matter as Reinforcement for Correct Mathematics,"[6] he learned that music was so reinforcing that it could have strong transfer effects to other subjects. Similarly, in his 1976 study, "Choice of Televised Music Lessons Versus Free Play in Relationship to Academic Improvement,"[7] he observed that children preferred to learn about music rather than play independently, when given the choice. Academic growth was always an important value for Clifford, consistent with his having grown up in a household with educators as parents. Clifford is tenacious in his quest to help children develop academically. In his very favorite research study, published in 1988, "The Use of Music in Cross-Age Tutoring Within Special Education Settings,"[8] fifth-graders tutored kindergarten students with special needs. Clifford discussed why this was his favorite study:

> It's my favorite study because it demonstrates that a simple pairing, with appropriate age differences, of older and younger students can have such an effect. The personal involvement and attachment of the older and younger students is heartening. The study demonstrates more than any other I've done how, when put in the right situation, older students can truly "act their way into a new way of thinking."
>
> (Madsen, Clifford. Personal Interview. 12 December 2018)

Clifford was equally tenacious in his research endeavors when examining ways in which students could remain engaged in subject matter.

> The research strongly indicates that one of the most important things for the student is to be engaged. And it doesn't matter if they are engaged in football or music or any other school activity. But they need to have a reason to get up and go to school. And that's the engagement, that's the

> passion. And I think that for some people, it's our bands and orchestras and choruses that really provide that entity. That a kid wants to get up and go to school. Why? Because, you know, "at the end of the day I get to go to chorus and sing, and that is a special experience."
>
> (Madsen, Clifford. Personal Interview. 1 July 2015)

Clifford enfolds his positive behavioral approach into his teaching, research, and service. He endeavors to teach others how to enrich their own lives, using their own value systems, by taking charge of their decisions. Identifying behaviors rather than vague ideas is one step toward making these changes. And, as he has stated repeatedly, "The biggest single indicator of future behavior is past and present behavior" (Madsen, Clifford. Personal Interview. 1 July 2015).

Making Decisions Based on Data

"Assumptive mode is the enemy."

From his childhood days, Clifford was a very curious person. Growing up with parents who were both educators, he developed an affinity for asking questions, looking for answers, and figuring out how things worked. Undergirding his love of learning was his desire to seek methods to discover truth. Perhaps as a result of his years on the school debate team, one way in which he sought answers to difficult questions was to consider both sides of an issue and attempt to present them convincingly, such that all elements were considered carefully. He implemented this practice into his College Teaching in Music course, wherein his graduate students engaged in debates about critical issues in higher education, including professor evaluation practices, accreditation, elements of the college admittance process, and tenure/promotion criteria. In most cases, he would assign the topic that was least congruent with the student's actual beliefs (if he knew what they were), for the specific purpose of getting them to present a viewpoint alternative to their own in a convincing manner.

Clifford believed that, rather than thinking on a surface level before deciding something, people should avail themselves of the data that is present and relevant to that decision. A strong advocate for the work of Consumers Union, he will often purchase annual subscriptions for family members and loved ones. He takes great care when making purchasing decisions to check *Consumer Reports* and read their recommendations.

> I remember buying a *Consumer Reports* subscription for my sweet mom. Year after year, I'm sending that to her and hoping that she'd be

> informed. So, I went there one time and she needed to get a new fridge or whatever and I said, "Where's your *Consumer Reports*?" She said, "Oh, it's out there, somewhere." I thought, "Oh, well. . . ."
>
> I mean, the *Consumer Reports* auto testing facilities is many times bigger than anything else in the world. They have such a loyal database that you can pick up *Consumer Reports*, buy a used car, and it will say, "If it has over these many miles, you're probably going to have to replace this part." . . . Now why would anybody go buy a used car without availing themselves of those data? It's just hard for me to get my mind around. I mean, people spend more time trying to decide what microwave they want, and they cost less than a hundred bucks now. And yet, they'll go into a new environment and give themselves a day and a half with a realtor to buy a house that costs $250 to $275,000. On what basis? Somebody telling them these are where the good schools are? "Well, I just like this, and I like the pantry." . . . It's hard for me not to be annoyed with people who should know better.
>
> (Madsen, Clifford. Personal Interview. 19 June 2015)

In his Psychology of Music class, which is taught to both undergraduate and graduate students and serves as an introduction to research class for them, Clifford discusses the three modes of inquiry, as defined in his *Experimental Research in Music* workbook and presented earlier in Chapter 4.[9] The first mode of inquiry is phenomenological. In this mode, one is not looking for proof of a given belief; rather, the belief is true irrespective of data. Some of the most important elements of life fall under this category. For example, he tells his students that, if someone were to ask him why he loves his wife Mary, he might answer with something that references her artistry in painting, the fact that she is a fantastic mother, or that she is a wonderful teacher. Yet, in reality, if Mary were none of these things, he would still love her. Thus, his love for Mary is phenomenological, and does not require empirical testing. The second mode of inquiry is the assumptive mode. In this mode, sometimes delineated visually as A:. BC (A is true, therefore B and C follow), one assumes a truth and then looks for data to prove that belief rather than staying open to whatever the data actually reveal. In the last mode of inquiry, hypothetical [(A) BC:. A], the researcher questions a hypothesis, seeks data, then draws conclusions based on the evidence collected, even if those conclusions are different than the original hypothesis. Clifford believes that these modes have utility in sorting out potential biases when approaching research questions.

When asked what he believes are the ten most important principles he wishes to share with his students, he mentions one related to his view that empiricism is important, but still, there are many important and powerful experiences in the world that cannot easily be measured in this way:

> So, I'm still thinking about what the biggest ten would be and I think one would subsume all of it, is to become more empirical or empirically oriented. And yet at the same time, some of the things that give art and music its greatest pizzazz are not the things that can be empirically tested.
>
> (Madsen, Clifford. Personal Interview. 19 June 2015)

Another important principle he wishes to impart is that research is a useful tool for life decisions. He recognizes that this approach is not always easy.

> [U]sing the benefits of research to inform your life. And of course, nobody wants to do that because a lot of the things, religion versus science or whatever . . . that's been a conflict that goes back forever. I was really happy that the Pope, chemist by training, just recently came out really strong on man-made pollution in our environment. And that's going to make a lot of people unhappy, especially the ones who are benefiting fiscally from these awful policies.
>
> (Madsen, Clifford. Personal Interview. 19 June 2015)

Acknowledging that quantitative researchers can sometimes fixate on statistical results and miss the larger goal of designing good studies and asking good research questions, Clifford says:

> Well, if truth lies in the .05 level of anything, then we are in really deep trouble. But the problem, I have been saying again and again and again . . . given time, form always trumps substance. And we forget why we are doing research in the first place.
>
> (Madsen, Clifford. Personal Interview. 19 June 2015)

This concept that "form always trumps substance" has been a concern of Clifford's for a long time. Clifford wrote the article "No One Knows Research But Me" in 1976.[10] In the article, which he wrote "tongue in cheek," he pointed out some of the silly ways in which some people in the field critique research but do not actually engage in it. He wrote:

> There are certain well-established rules for different areas of research. Unfortunately, many researchers argue these rules when they ought to be arguing different and/or collective modes of inquiry. For example, study of statistics often provides more concern for interpretive minutiae

> than illuminating information. Students often develop more concern for complex statistical interactions than for methodological rigor, or more concern for methodology than for the most important consideration, which should always be the importance of the variables under investigation.
>
> (170)

> Truth, musical or otherwise, does not rest at the .05 level. While we should try as hard as possible to play by the rules (i.e., the use of numbers demands rigorous constraints intended to minimize Type I and II errors lest we be grossly misled), we should also realize that inferential statistics constitute only a minor aspect of experimental research. It would indeed be encouraging if more research were rejected because of importance concerning the variable under question or methodological deficiencies rather than the use of the "wrong multiple range test," "inappropriate error term," or even "lack of random assignment."
>
> (178)

> Indeed, it is hoped that we never perpetuate our own research to the exclusion of thought or in any other way reinforce our own behavior to the point where we truly believe that "no one knows research but me."
>
> (180)

Clifford has a true love affair with research, and serves as an excellent model for his students to emulate. His passion for research is always present, and he will frequently come to his class to share some information he recently learned. He subscribes to over 25 research journals, as varied as *Review of Educational Research*, *Science*, and *The Skeptical Inquirer*. For Clifford, research and teaching are inextricably linked. He uses data for his own decision making, and encourages his students to do the same. His record of mentoring doctoral students (he has served as major professor to 92 students as of 2019; see the Appendix) is indicative of his enthusiasm for teaching and guiding research. Many of his doctoral students have continued to be leaders in the profession. He has instilled in them a strong desire to continue to be productive through their own love of research. See Chapter 7 for more about his professional legacy.

When asked about his guiding principles for mentorship, he relays his belief that doctoral students should be nurtured in a positive environment so that as a top priority, they are encouraged to continue in their research endeavors. It is less important, at least at first, that they do everything perfectly. The development of enthusiasm for research, thus learning, is primary.

> Well, I tried one time actually to have a formal research thing once a week. And it works really well for about six or seven weeks and the idea was that a faculty member would present her or his research or a doctoral student would. . . . But it was under the "let's be positive." Not like the model, "let's hear and tear everybody down." But let's be positive. And, say, "Well, I think that you might want to change this because, you know, you would be embarrassed if somebody were to ask you about it. For example, you attempt to control for order effect, you don't control for order, you just attempt to do that. You don't really know." Those kind of things. And, it's just like teaching somebody how to pronounce a word correctly. You might say, "It's transgender. It's not transgendered. And it's Reform Jewish, not Reformed Jewish." And those are just little things but those are the things that can get people in trouble when they are out of their own bubble, as it were, or their own habitat.
>
> (Madsen, Clifford. Personal Interview. 25 June 2015)

Clifford's positive approach to teaching research, and everything else, is consistent with his positive behavioral approach.

Transfer

> "Well, as you know, everything relates to everything."

In his Senior Researcher Award address, Clifford Madsen wrote, "It seems to me that the most important education issues relate to a person's ability to make transfers."[11] True understanding of a given topic requires the person to recognize the same idea across numerous examples or contexts. Clifford was always troubled by the fact that individuals did not transfer on their own accord, so he set out immediately to teach students to transfer across all of his courses. Clifford recalls the first moment he began teaching for transfer in an applied trumpet lesson, during which one of his students was struggling with the harmonic minor melodic line in an etude for trumpet.

> And I said, "Did you take theory?" He said, "Yeah, straight As . . . four semesters." And I said, "You did all the minor scales?" He says, "Yeah." I said, "Well, did you study harmonic minor?" . . . Ab . . . B nat. . . . He said, "Oh!" And so in that instant, I made up my mind to do something that worked beautifully from that day to this. I said, "Okay, what I want you to do is to find something that you're studying in your other music classes that directly relates to my assignment for your applied lesson."
>
> (Madsen, Clifford. Personal Interview. 12 May 2015)

From that lesson forward, he began asking his trumpet students to do a variety of things in their lessons, including composition, because this activity required a high level of transfer. One of his early trumpet students recalls:

> This is another example of how . . . how advanced Cliff was and how beyond his basic role as a trumpet teacher . . . he did creative and clever things. Like, for example, he had us all write a trumpet etude! We had to come up with a trumpet etude, and we all played our little etudes in front of, guess who, composition faculty, and they picked a winner of the best composition!
>
> (Forsythe, Jere. Personal Interview. 12 April 2015)

Clifford believes that many issues in life can be attributed to a lack of the ability to transfer, which results in the individual repeatedly making the same mistakes. How can one become independent without the ability to transfer?

> I mean the best thing that a jazz person could possibly do is say okay, Monday morning, Friday night concert, wonderful. I've got six new charts up there. You're going to take 5 minutes and I want everybody here to find at least six things in the new charts that we worked on in those old charts, cause if we don't do that it's just a new chart and we just start all over again.
>
> (Madsen, Clifford. Personal Interview. 12 May 2015)

As previously mentioned, Clifford incorporates a transfer activity at the start of every class period. He enters his classroom and immediately says, "Take out a sheet of paper and write a transfer." Students begin to write about anything they choose as long as it involves some type of near or far transfer. This daily activity stretches the students to continually attempt to transfer, which Clifford also models regularly. When we asked his former students what they learned from studying with Dr. Madsen, most, if not all, reference transfer.

> The value of and learning how to think . . . higher-order teaching skills, learning skills, conceptual skills, and . . . transfer, transfer, transfer. Well, they're all first cousins, if not the same thing. But I learned how to do that, mostly because it was being modeled, not because I was told to.
>
> (Johnson, Christopher. Personal Interview. 16 March 2016)

Storytelling, or vicarious teaching, is also a trademark of Clifford's teaching that promotes student transfer. Many former students vividly recall stories that were told to the class to teach a concept or life lesson. "My favorite stories are the ones when I learned to transfer. Being in Cliff's class is a little like sitting in church listening to parables or reading *Aesop's Fables*; it's the stories that help you connect with the information" (Juchniewicz, Jay. Personal Interview. 4 May 2016).

"The Green Life Saver" is one example of a story frequently referenced by his students. In this story, a young child comes up to Clifford following a presentation to offer him a very special Life Saver candy that the child has been saving in his pocket. The child lovingly gifts the Life Saver, which is covered with lint and dirt, to Clifford. Clifford graciously accepts the candy, saying, "Oh, how sweet. Thank you so very much. I will keep this safe and enjoy it later." Of course, the "green Life Saver" is a metaphor for someone offering something to you that may have little inherent value on the surface, and perhaps may even be a nuisance. To that child or person, the green Life Saver is a treasure that they have offered you. There is no reason to scorn or belittle another person who is offering you a gift. It may be the only thing they have to offer. "Always take the green Life Saver!" says Clifford. The stories told in Clifford's classes, or in his office, were never told for the sake of the story or for entertainment, but for the lesson that was embedded within the story.

> My favorite Dr. Madsen lessons were not stories he shared during class. My favorite stories were shared with me after Michael Allen passed away. In our conversations, he shared many stories about our friend that will stay with me forever. However, when sharing those stories with me, Dr. Madsen managed to transfer the stories' lessons into my life in an effort to help me grow as a person.
>
> (Pope, David. Personal Interview. 19 June 2016)

Without transfer, content knowledge may be lost. During his Psychology of Music class, Clifford teaches the standard statistical tests frequently used by quantitative researchers. For each of these statistical tests, students are required to conduct mini experiments in which they transfer their knowledge of the targeted statistical test: chi square, Mann Whitney U, and t-test. He insists that students conduct their own statistical analyses by hand, so that they can understand what is happening with the raw numbers and avoid arbitrary searches for statistical significance. Of even more importance is the individual's ability to read and transfer the results of research into their daily lives.

> Transfer also seems to be the key to gaining greater meaning from research reports as well as all other reading, and I have suggested that until each of us as a professional is capable of answering the important

> question of how this information can relate to us, it is probably fruitless to seek any easy solutions to our many problems.[12]

Suffice it to say that without transfer, little of what we do has meaning beyond that moment. Clifford endeavored to help his students transfer so that they could become empowered, independent, and happy.

Happiness

> "We are what we repeatedly do."
>
> (Durant)

> "The mind is everything. What you think, you become."
>
> (Buddha)

Two of Clifford Madsen's favorite quotes are "We are what we repeatedly do," and "What you think, you become." Clifford has been contemplating philosophy ever since his mother gifted him Durant's *The Story of Philosophy: The Lives and Opinions of the Great Philosophers of the Western World.*[13] We live the majority of our life in our own mind. From Clifford's point of view, what we choose to think and replay becomes who we are. "I think everybody has two stories, like I had in that sociology class, no matter what their situation is. And they can either concentrate on the bad and rehearse that. . . . Or, they can choose to rehearse the good" (Madsen, Clifford. Personal Interview. 2 September 2018).

Rumination is an affliction with which many people grapple. On a very basic level, this is what Clifford is trying to help others avoid: repeating the same negative thoughts over and over, the same negative experience or failure over and over, or the slight received by another person over and over, especially as these repetitions tend to distort the reality of the initial experience. If one is going to replay events, why not choose the positive events: the time one received a compliment, the jury in which one performed well on one's instrument, a kindness bestowed upon one by another? If in fact, humans avoid pain and seek pleasure, one of his academic epiphanies while reading *Utilitarianism* by John Stuart Mill, then why would individuals choose to replay negative events?

> There will be enough suffering that comes into everyone's life just growing up. People don't ever have to go looking for it, and the thing that bothers me the most is people as they age choose to suffer, then turn that vice into a virtue—the mental rehearsal of all the slights that people have endured from others.
>
> (Madsen, Clifford. Personal Interview. 2 September 2018)

Helping others to change their own patterns of thinking is a gift that he bestows on his students. In *Teaching/Discipline*, there is a story of a mother awaiting errant progeny:

> Mother has just finished teaching and expects her seventeen-year-old son to pick her up from school at approximately 4:00 P.M. Four arrives, and no son; the woman attempts to call him but he doesn't answer his phone. She begins to pace a little and thinks about a hectic afternoon and a ruined supper. At 4:15 P.M. she is still trying to reach him. She becomes a little angry and thinks about her inconsiderate offspring. Four-thirty P.M. arrives, and, in spite of trying to do something else, she begins to worry about his where-abouts. Between 5:45 P.M. and 6:00 P.M. (while many transportation invitations are turned down and many attempts to reach him fail) he is imagined dead in a car wreck, attacked by someone, unconscious in the hospital, picked up by the police, drunk in an alley, and sundry other things, all of which are negative (she has even lost her concern for transportation). Is it not strange that during these times most people do not imagine that the son simply forgot the time? What, in reality, is the problem in this case? The mother who is "fretting and worrying" about possible catastrophic events, or a seventeen-year-old-son who is late? One real problem is worry.[14]

The reason that the mother's worrying is more problematic than the tardy son is because worry is very punishing to the person who engages in the act, not to the others who may be the object of worry or frustration. Worry then results in a form of self-punishment. Clifford Madsen encourages students to train their minds to avoid worrying, and discourages them from reinforcing the act of worry in others by limiting the time they spend listening to loved ones ruminate.

> There was this program, came on at 12 o'clock. It was called *Queen for a Day*. And they'd have these three old sisters and they'd get up and go public about how they'd suffered. "I've suffered more than you've suffered." And they had their stories of woe. And they'd say, "Let's hear it for contestant number 1." And the applause meter went on (*claps*), "Number 2!" (*claps*), "Number 3!" (*claps and screams*). They get this awful-looking tiara, whatever it is . . . a year's supply of Tide soap. Queen for a Day.
>
> (Madsen, Clifford. Class Lecture. 12 June 2015)

The celebration of suffering turns a vice into a virtue. Why do people choose to suffer, or to relive suffering? Clifford shares:

> The research shows that people who lived through the Holocaust and were reasonably able to put it down and live through it are the only ones who were happy; rehearsing misery is a problem. Part of happiness is to move on. Everyone has bad things and good things. If you focus on the bad things and rehearse those, that is what you become.
>
> (Madsen, Clifford. Personal Interview. 2 September 2018)

One way that he encourages students to view their lives differently, and hopefully in a positive direction, is by having them compare their own life experience to those with less fortune.

> And so, for example, for the last two or three years, I've just gone up on the board and I said, "Why is it so hard to structure," and I'd write down this line. This is the top, most wonderful thing that's ever happened or could happen to you, in your mind's eye. This is the worst thing that's ever happened to you (different line). This is the worst thing that's ever happened to the human condition (lowest line). This is the worst thing that's happened to you. And right away people look at that and say, "Oh my goodness." A lot of them, you know, it's like going to church and saying "I'm so fortunate" and "I'm so blessed," "I'm so . . ." because they just, they realize that the worst thing that ever happened in their lives is often better than the best thing that happened in other people's lives and that's really hard to get your mind around.
>
> (Madsen, Clifford. Personal Interview. 19 May 2015)

One of the most impactful lectures that Clifford delivers to his Behavior Modification class is "Who Claps for You?" This lecture is selected by many of his former students as the most meaningful of the lessons they learn from Clifford Madsen. The lecture regularly occurs near the end of the term, after students have spent the majority of the semester learning about behavior management techniques. In this lecture, Clifford flips the student's perspective from the one in control of delivering approval and disapproval to the one receiving the feedback.

> **Excerpts From "Who Claps for You?"**
>
> Today's class is "Who claps for you?"
>
> I have to tell you my story because it starts with my wonderful, lovely mother. We had a big family. Smart Mom. She taught me how to do everything, how to take care of myself, how to take care of my little sisters, wash, cook. She taught independence and she taught life skills

that were important. Good. Thank you, Mom. She also taught me how to be very, very compliant. Compliant.

The very first time I went to school, I'm all excited about new shoes, and on the way out my mother said, "What are you going to do to get the teacher to like you?" I said, "I dunno." She said, "You'll think of something."

Well, she always followed through. So I got home that night and she said, "Well, how did it go?" and I said, "Well it went, you know, very well." And she said, "Well what did you do to get the teacher to like you?" And I said "Mom, I couldn't think of anything. I couldn't think of anything." She said "Well, did you put your materials away when the teacher . . ." "Uh huh." "Well did you line up?" "Uh huh." "Well that's a start. You'll think of something."

Years later, I was given the opportunity to babysit for another family. When I was getting ready to go babysit, my mother sits me down, locks eyes, and says "Clifford, do you understand the nature of this work?" "Eh?" "Do you understand why you're going to Mrs. Whiting's house?" "Well yeah, to babysit." "NO! You're there to ensure that those two children remain alive. You may NOT go to sleep, you may NOT talk on the phone. If you go to sleep, you're just another liability in there. Now if a fire breaks out, we have four people instead of three."

Well, I had my marching orders. And I did what she told me. I was very compliant. Wouldn't have occurred to me not to be. So, I got to the Whitings', read the kids a story, gave them their bath and put them in bed. I know how to do that, that was easy stuff. But my mother had also said on the way out, "Oh and Clifford, make sure you do something extra." Extra. Okay. So after I got the kids in bed, I went into the kitchen and obviously they had entertained because the place was just filled with dirty dishes. "Great, I got it! I'll clean this up!" And I did.

The Whitings came home and I heard this shriek from the kitchen, and then Mrs. Whiting came out and whispered something to Dr. Whiting and he reached back into his pocket and came back with his wallet again. I was smart enough to figure out what was going on here. And then she said, "Clifford, you did these dishes" and I said, "Yes ma'am." She said, "That's wonderful." And I knew that I had a gig. Little something extra, Clifford.

But the problem was that it generalized, and we've talked about generalizing in this class before. What's the problem with generalization? It includes everything. It's non-discriminating. Is that good? No!

So, compliance. Is that good? Well of course it's good. Unless it's not.

The whole point today is "Who claps for you?" Anybody? Everybody? What if they are not nice people? And they can get into our guts.

> Why do we give them that power? Roommates that we don't even like wreck our whole day by saying, "You're going to wear *that* today?" We've already decided they have no taste whatsoever. Why does it bother us? People in your family that keep asking you inappropriate questions that should not ever be asked because it's not their business. "When are we going to hear some of those wedding bells?" Followed quickly by "Sure would like to hear some pattering feet." It's none of their business. And why can they hurt us? Why do we give them that power?
>
> I grew up in a church where the entire congregation would sing and every once in a while, I was standing right next to my dad in church, I think I told you before, somewhere between strict and free organum. I mean it (his voice) would change pitch, barely. And I'd think (in an annoyed tone) "oh, softer." Of course, later on, I was ashamed of myself. Stupid, immature [me], I'm sitting there worried about his pitch, and his volume. He's very proud of me. And he never missed the opportunity to say, "Clifford makes that trumpet talk. He can make that trumpet talk." Well he wouldn't know if the trumpet was talking, walking, or in a daze. You think I should go to him for my musical feedback? Of course not. Sweet, wonderful man, but he couldn't hear. He didn't know. He was so bad that he didn't even know that he didn't know. But he loved me. Yay. Much more important than his musical critique. Thank you, Dad.
>
> So, who claps for you. . . . Everybody? When's the last time you thought about that?
>
> See, today, we're talking about something that is antithetical to everything we have talked about in this class up to this day. Everything we've talked about up to this point in time is: You are in charge, you're the one who decides. And now I'm asking you to think about "Who's in charge of you? Who claps for you? For whom do you want to clap? Everybody?"
>
> You're thinking about it . . . good. Many people say it's the most important day in this class. So, who claps for you? I suggest folks, you have way too many people that you allow to clap for you. And by definition, what does that mean? People who clap for you are people who can hurt you, but it never starts out that way.
>
> (Madsen, Clifford. Class Lecture. 12 June 2015)

From Clifford Madsen's point of view, to some degree, happiness is a choice. Replaying positive events, viewing your life in a larger perspective, and choosing who gets to "clap for you" are key elements of finding happiness. The final piece is how one chooses to spend one's time.

> [J]ust seeing people get really excited and become really happy with what they're doing on a day-to-day basis that makes them happy and makes other people happy. So, that's how I would hope success is measured, for the most part, by the individual who is living the life.
>
> (Madsen, Clifford. Personal Interview. 29 June 2015)

Time Is Life

> "Our greatest difficulty is that we cannot tell time."

Clifford began writing the unpublished manuscript *Life's Time* in 1970. He has been contemplating the issue of time for many, many years. At the surface level, being mindful of time and how time is used allows him to stay productive and maximize his efficiency. However, when thinking about time in a more in-depth way, Clifford believes time is intimately related to life and human relationships. Indeed, time is life. His fascination with time is really a fascination with getting the very most out of life, so that all may have high-magnitude, high-intensity experiences as often as possible. It is important to him to "take out the clutter," and that is true for cluttering communication with loved ones, for taking time with children, and for having quality time with others.[15]

> Benjamin Franklin says "don't squander time because that's the stuff of life." And it seems to me that most of us don't have nearly the amount of intensity or magnitude out of our life experiences that we ought to have.[16]

Frequency versus magnitude is a principle that has received a lot of Clifford's attention. As a subsection in *Life's Time*, and later inserted as a chapter in the fifth edition of *Teaching/Discipline*, he wrote about the difference between the two terms and how differentiation is closely tied to happiness and depression:

> It must be also recognized that some people seem to be incapable of high magnitude of feeling or emotion because they continuously *substitute frequency for magnitude*. These people are incapable of intense human interactions and therefore substitute numerous shallow and meaningless encounters. This scheme of substituting frequency for magnitude does not seem to be productive especially in the long run. Indeed, much behavior falls into the category of attempting to substitute frequency for magnitude. There are people whose daily lives are filled with meaningless and inconsequential human encounters so inane

> as not to be remembered. Sometimes people do not limit this banal behavior to encounters with persons with whom they come in cursory contact but also to their "significant others" (i.e., husband, wife, friend, partner, relative) where one would hope that they would desire more consequential and in-depth relationships. If frequent but superficial interactions were relegated to those situations where we desire nothing more, then there would be no problem. However, when we are incapable of intense deep relationships with those few people about whom we truly ought to care, then the situation becomes pathetic. These sad human encounters are characterized by constant repeated attempts at intensity yet a continual failure to provide anything of a magnitude such that the encounter cannot be remembered, let alone provide even minimal personal fulfillment.
>
> In understanding life's time, frequency in relationship to magnitude is *extremely* consequential. Depression as a lifestyle can be intense, frequent, and catastrophic. It is difficult to imagine any long-standing depression of extreme magnitude that has not been reinforced with great frequency to the point that it becomes self-destructive. Alternately, there are the happy times where magnitude is obviously increased by frequency. If such times transcend the short-term pleasurable events that one may experience daily, then fun may eventually turn to satisfaction. Intense physiological reactions can be brought about on the joyful as well as the depressive side. In our cyclic lifestyle, intensity relates to frequency and frequency to intensity. There can be a growing reinforcement of those behaviors that lead to the amelioration of life's time or conversely, of those behaviors which are destructive of life's time (if not also of life itself). While it is readily apparent that the factor of magnitude in a lifestyle must be analyzed in relationship to frequency, it is also apparent that frequency can exist apart from magnitude and truly pathetic people seem to be those whose lives are characterized by total frequency as opposed to in-depth or meaningful experience (magnitude).[17]

As mentioned in Chapter 4, in his Behavior Modification course, Clifford asks his students to keep a time log for one week. The assignment is intended to get them to think about their values and the ways in which those values align with their time usage. They begin by designating their top five values, and then he asks them to log every activity in which they engage (including sleep), in half-hour intervals, for a full week (seven days). On the last page, he asks them to now reflect again on those five values, and determine whether those values are indeed still held, or if they have changed. The question is intended to be a bit tongue-in-cheek, but thought-provoking nonetheless. As is often the case, many students will claim that "this week was just not typical." To that, he asks them to take data on a different week, whereupon most will discover that there is no real construct of a typical week.

Another concept that Clifford emphasizes in his Behavior Modification course is scheduling of reinforcement. These schedules are well documented in the psychology and behavioral literature. He references them in his *Life's Time* book to further elucidate how structuring time allows for greater happiness.

> A useful technique in the analysis of a problem situation of any human behavior is to contrive an experiment whereby we could produce a behavior that we are trying to understand or analyze. In this sense we may ask ourselves the question, "How would we produce a gambler?" Or, how would we get someone "hooked" on gambling? Alternately, how might we get someone hooked on reading books or how might we get one hooked on generosity or depression? Setting up a situation whereby we could get someone to be a gambler appears quite easy. Obviously, we would want the person to enjoy success initially. We would set up a situation whereby we invite our potential gambler to come to the place where gambling could occur. Next, we might want to model for this person some kind of pleasurable response—winning. It might be useful to have someone in the person's view "hit the jackpot" or in some other way demonstrate the obvious "joys" of gambling. We might begin by giving our person some money with which to gamble or in some other way ensure that gambling begins. Perhaps one of the most difficult questions to be asked is, "How do you get someone to initially engage in a behavior such that it is possible to reinforce that behavior?" Indeed, sometimes it is not possible to get one to engage in the initial behavior in which case that behavior can never be reinforced! If we do succeed in getting the gambler to begin gambling, then we would set up a fixed schedule whereby the person wins initially. Yet quite quickly we would want to set up a *variable schedule* whereby the gambler would start to lose a little yet still desire to persist. Various reinforcement schedules could be designed which would almost certainly ensure the continuance of gambling behavior (if indeed this represents our value system) by manipulating the external contingencies in the environment of the gambler. If we know the person who we are trying to get to gamble, it makes it easier for us to set up the schedule of reinforcement that would structure persistence. The major notion here is that we are capable of *experimentally conjecturing* with some high probability of success the creation of gambling

behavior. Alternately, in this same regard we can apply knowledge of reinforcement schedules in order to understand a person who is already a compulsive gambler.

Now let us examine schedules of reinforcement concerning mental depression. If depression is defined as negative verbal interactions and accompanying physiological states having to do with worry and one's lamenting about one's condition, then using this behavioral definition it is possible for us to create an imagined "experiment." Suppose in this situation that we seek to create a person reinforced for depressive behavior to the point of complete incapacitation. The important ingredient again would concern schedules of reinforcement. Using the above gambling model, the first thing that we would want our potentially depressive person to do would be to win concerning negative thoughts. Perhaps the easiest way to do this would be to find someone in this person's environment that would not only elicit, but reinforce to a high degree, the person's negative feelings expressed in verbalization concerning how bad life is or how bad a particular situation is. After the initial reinforcement is established we would then want to put this person on some kind of partial reinforcement schedule whereby we could teach this person to persist with these negative verbalizations. It would be unwise to use a fixed schedule. For example, on a fixed interval schedule a person could only speak about negative things one day a week or five minutes each day. Therefore, this type of schedule might actually make the depression "silly" and be used to *decrease* negative verbalization concerning life's misery. Actually, a variable schedule concerning responses about life's misery reinforced at odd times and with varying *frequency and magnitude* would be much better. Verbalizations, thoughts, and feelings concerning how "bad life really is" could be subjected to effective schedules of reinforcement. Experimentally then, we could create someone who, over a period of time, would become more and more depressed. Thus, we can specify a *reinforcement schedule* such that it explains those conditions that contribute to depressive behavior. Obviously, if there are chemical reasons for depression it becomes more complicated. However, more and more situations can be devised using schedules of reinforcement to understand how across time a person actually develops the behaviors that we wish to investigate.[18]

The entire goal of understanding the reinforcement schedules that we are subjected to and inadvertently create for ourselves is to provide not only understanding for the restructuring of schedules that cause the most harm, but also to establish alternative schedules that cause the

> greatest joy. . . . If we can understand the subtle schedules that influence our lives, then for the most part we can restructure those schedules so that they will contribute to our happiness.[19]

In 1965, Clifford wrote the poem "I'll Be Happy Tomorrow," which captures many of his thoughts regarding time, and that time is life.

> Come soft end of labored day
> Come short time with joyful play
> Come patterned sunlight enticing pay
> Come cleavage break of my dismay
> I'll be happy tomorrow
>
> If small courage I could find
> If laser acids masked benign
> If once ahead and not behind
> If given time to help mankind
> I'll be happy tomorrow
>
> When just a little I have stored
> When new game points have next been scored
> When talents' worth won't be ignored
> When justly freed I can't be bored
> I'll be happy tomorrow
>
> Will the hurt then come to end
> Will at last a temporal friend
> Will deserving love transcend
> Will my grief yet finally spend
> I'll be happy tomorrow
>
> Come that time when I reply
> If truth my value cannot imply
> When I pursue and find out why
> Will I choose still to live the lie
> I'll be dead tomorrow.

Notes

1. Madsen, Clifford K., and Charles H. Madsen, Jr. *Teaching/Discipline: A Positive Approach for Educational Development*. 5th ed. Raleigh, NC: Contemporary Publishing Company of Raleigh, 2016.
2. Bennett, Barbara. *Oral Memoirs of Clifford K. Madsen*. Institute for Oral History, Baylor University, 2000. P. 48.

3. Mill, John Stuart. *Utilitarianism*. London: Fraser's Magazine, 1861.
4. Madsen, Clifford K., and Charles H. Madsen, Jr. *Teaching/Discipline: A Positive Approach for Educational Development*. 5th ed. Raleigh, NC: Contemporary Publishing Company of Raleigh, 2016. P. 61.
5. Madsen, Clifford K., et al. *Research in Music Behavior: Modifying Music Behavior in the Classroom*. New York: Teachers College Press, 1975.
6. Madsen, Clifford K. "The Effect of Music Subject Matter as Reinforcement for Correct Mathematics." *Bulletin of the Council for Research in Music Education*, vol. 59, no. 59, 1979. Pp. 54–58.
7. Madsen, Clifford K., and John M. Geringer. "Choice of Televised Music Lessons Versus Free Play in Relationship to Academic Improvement." *Journal of Music Therapy*, vol. 13, no. 4, 1976. Pp. 154–162.
8. Madsen, Clifford K., et al. "The Use of Music in Cross-Age Tutoring Within Special Education Settings." *Journal of Music Therapy*, vol. 25, no. 3, 1988. Pp. 135–144.
9. Madsen, Clifford K., and Randall S. Moore. *Experimental Research in Music: Workbook in Design and Statistical Tests*. Rev. ed. Raleigh, NC: Contemporary Pub., 1978.
10. Madsen, Clifford K. "No One Knows Research But Me." *Journal of Music Therapy*, vol. 11, no. 4, 1974. Pp. 169–180.
11. Madsen, Clifford K. "Senior Researcher Award Acceptance Address." *Journal of Research in Music Education*, vol. 36, no. 3, 1988. Pp. 135.
12. Madsen, Clifford K. "Senior Researcher Award Acceptance Address." *Journal of Research in Music Education*, vol. 36, no. 3, 1988. P. 135.
13. Durant, Will. *The Story of Philosophy: The Lives and Opinions of the Great Philosophers of the Western World*. 2nd ed. New York: Simon and Schuster, 1961.
14. Madsen, Clifford K., and Charles H. Madsen, Jr. *Teaching/Discipline: A Positive Approach for Educational Development*. 5th ed. Raleigh, NC: Contemporary Publishing Company of Raleigh, 2016. P. 9.
15. Bennett, Barbara. *Oral Memoirs of Clifford K. Madsen*. Institute for Oral History, Baylor University, 2000. P. 52.
16. Bennett, Barbara. *Oral Memoirs of Clifford K. Madsen*. Institute for Oral History, Baylor University, 2000. P. 49.
17. Madsen, Clifford K. *Life's Time*. Unpublished manuscript. n.d. P. 39.
18. Madsen, Clifford K. *Life's Time*. Unpublished manuscript. n.d. P. 53.
19. Madsen, Clifford K. *Life's Time*. Unpublished manuscript. n.d. P. 55.

Part III

Legacy

7 Clifford Madsen's Legacy

Life, Love, and Lessons Learned

Clifford Madsen has truly influenced the fields of education and music therapy, nationally and internationally. Because Clifford chose to view the world through a combination of philosophy, personal values, and data, we chose to write this last chapter as a research study in his honor. Therefore, and with much love, the purpose of this chapter is to examine the teachings of Clifford Madsen through the eyes of his former students and loved ones.

Between the years of 2015 and 2019, we interviewed Dr. Clifford Madsen; his wife, Mary; his children, Katia, Cort, and Sitka; 26 of his former doctoral students; and select acquaintances for the purpose of writing his biography. Additionally, 17 of his former graduate teaching assistants emailed us responses to our interview questions. The 26 former students who were interviewed in person were those who worked closely with Dr. Madsen in teaching-assistant capacities prior to 2002, and were selected based on their professional reputation in the field of music education or music therapy. We analyzed the transcripts of these interviews using an open-coding process as outlined by Saldaña.[1] A sample of the interview transcripts ($n = 5$) were independently coded and analyzed using in vivo quotes. Utilizing these quotes, we established themes and values related to what former students learned from Dr. Madsen. We reconciled the themes through extensive discussion. This process was repeated several times to establish intercoder reliability, as outlined by Campbell et al.[2]

Themes based on the analysis and reconciliation process emerged. Former students shared that Dr. Madsen fostered a love of learning in his students and a research mindset that encourages curiosity and discovery. He loved his students, was generous with his time, and urged those around him to be independent and make their own decisions. The most common lessons learned were values such as love, kindness, and generosity, and the ways in which time influences our lives, including productivity, focus of attention, and the frequency and magnitude of experiences. These lessons encouraged his students to establish their own personal values, increase their awareness of time, and make choices for themselves. Because he taught his students to transfer knowledge, his students gained the necessary skills to become independent.

Curiosity and a Research Mindset

Clifford is a very curious person. He still becomes excited when discovering new concepts or ideas. He shares his passionate search for knowledge with his students. In 2013, Hodges, Teachout, and Sink interviewed eminent music education scholars regarding their productivity. When asked about his incentives and motivations for sustaining scholarly output, Clifford wrote, "I've thought about this a lot and can only identify one issue, an insatiable curiosity about most everything and especially concerning music and teacher education. I just love doing research."[3]

Clifford instilled the need for curiosity in his students. During his interview, John Geringer described the most important thing he had learned from Clifford as "just the delight or joy of discovering things . . . doing studies. And doing a good job in the process" (Geringer, John. Personal Interview. 24 June 2015). Jane Cassidy shared, "[I learned] to be curious about everything. You know, if you are not curious about anything, you are never going to do anything important from a research standpoint" (Cassidy, Jane. Personal Interview. 3 June 2016).

Clifford insisted that his students consider their biases and assumptions before beginning a research endeavor. He taught his students three modes of inquiry—phenomenological, assumptive, and hypothetical (see Chapter 6)—so that they would be able to differentiate between what they believed and what they were truly willing to investigate. These modes were referenced by a number of his former students as a way to sort through their own views and beliefs, as well as topics they intended to study.

> The one thing that has made the most impact on me and my students are the ways of knowing. That knowledge, and empirically based knowledge, is different than belief. Cliff helped me realize that knowledge is a human construction. And his ways of knowing with empirical evidence versus assumptions versus belief-based or faith-based. Those were the big things.
>
> (Kuhn, Terry. Personal Interview. 1 June 2016)

Viewing the world through an empirical lens was revelatory to some of his students. "[Experimental Research] was an epiphany. It opened my eyes to the world of music from a scientific point of view. I can't tell you how exciting it was for me to have experienced that particular course!" (Wolfe, David. Personal Interview. 3 June 2016). Another student discussed the importance of curiosity with respect to opening possibilities.

> Clifford helped me to continue to grow my ability to be inquisitive—my curiosity. And he opened the possibility that I can do this. But also, what are the things that deserve to be questioned? Things that I never would've thought about before—he opened those doors to me. He never said to me, "You can't." There was never a closed door. He instilled possibilities.
>
> (Confredo, Deborah. Personal Interview. 16 March 2016)

Clifford was at the start of a research movement in music education and music therapy that valued empirical inquiry. As discussed in Chapter 3, conducting experimental research in music was somewhat new in the early 1970s.

> I think he was the pioneer; I think he was the original person that really did experimental research in music ed. I think he was the first person to say, "Okay, let's really—if we're talking about how to teach people, let's get an empirical basis for it." And for me, it was very important because I really wanted an empirical basis for it, too. I think he clearly did that: he developed a discipline in music education based on science that was not there before.
>
> (Greer, Doug. Personal Interview. 2 June 2016)

Values

Clifford's students felt that more than anything, they had learned through observation the value and importance of love, kindness, and generosity. Numerous students stressed the impact that Clifford made on them, both in and out of the classroom. Regardless of the subject matter of the particular course he was teaching, Clifford encouraged his students to develop their value system, and use that value system as a basis for making personal and professional decisions.

Love

Clifford Madsen loved his family, his students, and the pursuit of knowledge. When asked what lessons they learned from Clifford, former students asserted that two of the most important were love and kindness. Chris Johnson recalled that "he made sure—*all* the time—that he made every person around him feel welcomed and loved and accepted" (Johnson, Christopher. Personal Interview. 16 March 2016).

Clifford's relationship with his doctoral students extended beyond the classroom. He served as both model and mentor for his students. During the interviews, his former students reflected frequently about how much they had learned from Clifford simply by watching him model teaching, loving, giving, and researching.

> [I]n my particular case it's the modeling of teaching. Not so much how to teach but the enthusiasm about teaching, and wanting to teach, and certainly modeling for doing research and modeling for love of learning and modeling for being positive. Just all of those things.
>
> (Geringer, John. Personal Interview. 24 June 2015)

And he encouraged a love for learning by encouraging student independence:

> It became inspired learning. He always asked, "What do you want to work on?" I took all of his classes, of course. But there were also a lot of individual studies and research projects and reading programs that were self-devised. That was the most wonderful thing.
>
> (Flowers, Pat. Personal Interview. 23 June 2015)

New faculty members need to know much more than academic content to be successful navigating higher education and life. Clifford educated the entire person, and believed that to share a love of learning with a loved one is a most beautiful experience. He wrote an essay on the special relationship that revolves around a love of learning (see Figure 7.1).

Clifford made sure to show the people around him that he loved them, and made no apologies for doing so. He encouraged men to show their emotions.

> And, you know, Cliff Madsen is one of the first men who said "I love you" to me, including my dad and my grandfather. Cliff said, "I love you, sweet man," and kissed me on the cheek. And it was—I cried. I was like, "Okay. I'm okay here. I'm okay. I'm good. I can do this." And I did.
>
> (Williams, Lindsey. Personal Interview. 16 March 2016)

Clifford clearly loves his students. He models the values he believes in and helps his students become their very best.

Love of Learning

For years people have expressed the joy of life, of love, and, more particularly, love of learning. However, the most beautiful aspect of love, as far as learning is concerned, is to associate with loved ones in a learning situation. This relationship is not mentioned much historically mostly because many teacher-learning situations have been characterized as advisary or, at best, as protagonistic relationships. Contingencies of the learning process usually involve the student either trying to please the teacher or perhaps the teacher trying desparately to motivate the student to want to please the teacher if not actually to learn something.

Love relationships involving learning are much different: these unique and extremely rare human contacts are composed of two basic ingredients. First is the excitement emanating from the mutual discovery of a subject matter that is respected and loved by both teacher and student. Second is the love that gradually embraces all associated in this learning process. Personal contingencies of academic reinforcement are so internalized that to do less than one's best becomes inconceivable. Furthermore, to not notice the progressive yet ancillary social contingencies that accrue from peoples' studying together becomes more and more difficult until one day it is realized that the finest aspect of the relationship is the personal. This particular love of learning and its reverse, learning of love, through loved ones sharing a common experience is not a state of mind or even possible in most student-teacher encounters. It takes a great deal of time, long-term courage, short-term sensitivity, and, most important, appropriate modeling. And herein lies the crux of our pursuit.

In the beginning we should not be discouraged if we initially fail to love the rigor of our discipline or even if we become competitive and self-serving for as we mature we will be more able to act as though we truly love our subject and therefore as time passes to love one another.

Figure 7.1 Madsen's essay on a love of learning

> He has attributes that we all want. You know he's authentic. He is authentic in love. He made me a teacher. He made me a better person in love and in life. He made me deal with, gently, what issues would come. He chose me, along with all of us. He chose us, and then he loved us.
>
> (Codding, Peggy. Personal Interview. 24 March 2017)

Kindness

Love and kindness are related. Lecture after lecture, Clifford would include stories or reminders about the importance of kindness. One of the most frequently referenced stories was that of "the green Life Saver" (Chapter 6). Clifford would remind his students, "you always preserve human dignity."

> I mean, who teaches you to tell the good lie in order to preserve someone's dignity and spirit in a moment? And then, as a consequence of your action you get to leave that situation with grace and gratitude. Think about standing up for someone, but then understanding that there will be times when, in order to save a person's dignity, it is more important to stand with them. They don't need you to stand up for them, they need you to stand with them.
>
> (Madsen, Katia. Personal Interview. 15 April 2016)

Clifford would ask his class to consider first whether an individual was nice or kind when assessing that individual as a potential friend or significant other. One of his classroom activities was to consider one's exclusivity when considering whom to date. Rather than evaluating attractiveness, intelligence, or any number of attributes, Clifford would ask, "Is he kind? Is she kind? Are they kind?" He valued kindness, reinforced it in others, and modeled it constantly.

> I have never seen Cliff do anything that was ill-intended. I mean, he is fundamentally a kind, generous, grateful human being. That is the most important thing. And the fact that he is that, and is as successful as he is, is an object lesson for all of the people who think that those things are incompatible. So, to me, that is the most important thing (that I learned).
>
> (Duke, Robert. Personal Interview. 17 April 2016)

Wayne Goins recalled a time when Clifford described in class how one should respond when observing a given situation where someone is publicly embarrassing another individual, or—in some cases—the second person in question has unknowingly and inadvertently embarrassed themselves.

> You don't make a scene, you just help them de-escalate the situation. I just thought that was the most touching and sensitive and caring and nurturing thing. I thought it was beautiful. And I thought, that is a lifelong lesson to not only adopt for your own self, but to pass on to your children and our students and everybody who—you know, you want to teach them how to live the right way. I thought that was such a godly thing to do.
>
> (Goins, Wayne. Personal Interview. 5 June 2016)

Generosity

Clifford is an incredibly generous person, and it brings him great joy to help others. "To the very end and beyond, Cliff has extended himself—his wisdom, his knowledge, his generosity—to me over the years. And like I say, I would not be the person I am today without his input" (Wolfe, David. Personal Interview. 3 June 2016).

Clifford's financial generosity is somewhat astonishing. He is always sensitive to the fact that students are financially vulnerable during graduate school, and takes every opportunity to assist students in need. This generosity has sometimes taken the form of renting one of his houses to a graduate student for much less than market value, or of creating opportunities to pay students for various jobs. For example, preceding conferences, he would choose one graduate student to carry the FSU music faculty's research posters on the plane. After the conference, he would present the student with a check for providing that service. His generosity extended well beyond fiscal matters. Below are examples of what Clifford's former students had to share about his generosity:

> Cliff is one of the most generous people I know. He's generous in his time, giving what it takes for his students to become scholars, teachers, and friends. Time with Cliff led me to think more deeply and to ask penetrating questions about music, the music professions, and life. My life was made better because of knowing Cliff and by experiencing his generous spirit, commitment, and love.
>
> (Jellison, Judith. Personal Interview. 4 June 2016)

Clifford was available to his students—another way he showed his generosity. Most of his research productivity occurred during weekends and holidays because during business hours, he was always available for his students and colleagues.

> [I learned] to be generous with my time. I remember that Cliff would work . . . I don't know if he still does, but he used to work weekends. Any time I would go to school on the weekend, I would see his car in the parking lot, I would go into his office and have some kind of long conversation. Then when I got to LSU [Louisiana State University], I was trying to do the same thing for our graduate students here. I remember calling him, and I think I handwrote him a letter too, and just said, "I never knew what I was getting from you until I was gone and trying to give that experience [to] somebody else." I don't know how he got anything done when I was there, because I was in his office all the time.
>
> (Cassidy, Jane. Personal Interview. 3 June 2016)

Terry Kuhn shared a story about how Clifford purchased a suit for him for his first college interview because he didn't have the funds. He was nervous about the interview, and about the flight because he had never been on an airplane.

> I had never been on an airplane before I finished my Ph.D. And, airplanes were not that common a way of travel. I drove from Oregon to Florida three times before I ever flew it. But, I didn't know anything about how airlines or airplanes worked. . . . But, I figured it out and got the ticket and went to the airport that morning. I had an early morning flight to Washington . . . what was then called Washington National Airport. There was a chain-link fence that you walked on boards to get out to the plane on the tarmac. And, I was on that, between the two fences . . . narrow . . . and walking out. And I heard a voice, "Terry. . . ." And I thought, "Hell, nobody knows I am here. It must be me; I am the only one around." I turned around and there was Cliff. He was there. He didn't have anything in particular to say. He came to see me off and make sure that I was looking and feeling okay.
>
> (Kuhn, Terry. Personal Interview. 1 June 2016)

Frank Diaz also referenced Clifford's generosity, among many other strengths:

> I would not be who I am without Cliff. I wanted to be around this man, each and every day. He always had the ability to change his mind. . . . He always treated me as an adult and challenged me to think more deeply and to think smarter. From Cliff, I learned to be more loving and more generous, to treat people with more compassion, and to discriminate enough to know when to love contingently.
>
> (Diaz, Frank. Personal Interview. 14 March 2016)

When describing their mentor Clifford Madsen, his former students described him as loving, kind, and generous.

Time

Focus of Attention

Clifford made sure to keep his home and work lives separate. He made every effort to be on task. Whether it was focusing on his research, teaching, attending to the student in front of him, or spending time with his family, Clifford focused his entire being on that one thing. Work occurred during work hours at school, including weekends, but when he was home he focused on his family. His former students treasured his values regarding loved ones, and hoped to replicate those values in their own lives. "So, I think that I learned what a good marriage should look like. And what a good family person should be, because I have not really had a lot of that experience; I think I learned that from Cliff" (Greer, Doug. Personal Interview. 2 June 2016).

Clifford has this way of making you feel as though you were the most important thing to him at any given moment. Many of his acquaintances joked that everyone believed they were Clifford's favorite, because that is the way he made them feel. If he was visiting with you, he was on task to the conversation in that moment and never attempted to multitask, a skill that he believes does not exist.

> [Clifford made] you feel as though you were the most important thing to him at that moment. Nothing was more important than focusing on you and your learning and you as a person and you as a growing individual . . . it was just incredible!
>
> (Forsythe, Jere. Personal Interview. 1 June 2016)

Not only did Clifford focus his attention on individuals, but he also focused his attention on his work. His ability to focus was so keen that he wrote the entire first draft of *Teaching/Discipline* in 20 straight hours during a Christmas break, by hand. Not only does he possess the ability to remain on task, but he is also the master of engagement in the classroom. When one observes his classes, it is evident that he is aware of what every student is doing at every moment, and knows how to engage them such that they remain on task.

> And the ability to do that, then of course, he taught us—that it was all deliberate and that he was using a technique, for how you moved if people were beginning to flag in their attention, you move to the other side of the class, who you called on and why you called on them—that kind of very detailed explanation of how you got things to be the way they ought to be.
>
> (Prickett, Carol. Personal Interview. 28 April 2016)

Frequency and Magnitude

As described earlier, Clifford often referenced the distinction between frequency and magnitude. When thinking about spending quality time with loved ones, magnitude is far more important than frequency. Many of his students, including David Wolfe, remembered these lessons:

> Frequency versus magnitude in relationships. I can really speak to that now because my partner of 21 years passed away a couple of years ago and now I'm a single man. I'm going to be 71 next month, and so I'm faced now with being a single person. And . . . how important in the beginning—early relationships, whether they're friends that you might be, or maybe potential spouses or partners, whatever—but certainly frequency is important in the beginning to get to know that person. But as you begin to know that person, the intensity of that relationship—the magnitude of your interactions takes on more importance.
>
> (Wolfe, David. Personal Interview. 3 June 2016)

Productivity

Clifford's productivity, and that of his students, has been well documented. John Grashel conducted a study to examine the institutional affiliation and the university where the terminal degree was earned for authors of the *Journal of Research in Music Education* (JRME, the premier journal in the music education profession) from 1990 through 2005. Grashel also noted the same variables for the *JRME* Editors and Editorial Committee members during this same period. He concluded that FSU has been the most influential institution regarding publication in the *JRME* since 1990. In fact, FSU faculty and students were producers of 106 (25.4%) of the 418 articles published during this period. FSU awarded the doctorate to 19 members of the Editorial Committee of the *JRME*. Grashel observed:

> These data indicate that Florida State University has been the most influential institution regarding publication in the *Journal of Research in Music Education* since 1990. Clifford Madsen, first recipient of the Music Educators National Conference's "Senior Researcher" award, has led Florida State to its pre-eminent position in music education research through his, his colleagues', and his students' contribution to the research literature as published in the *JRME*. . . . In summary, the impact of Florida State University on the research agenda of the music education profession over the past 15 years is consequential. The work of the faculty, graduates, and students of Florida State have served as an example that might provide a model for other graduate institutions granting graduate degrees in music education to emulate.[4]

Of the 16 Senior Researcher awards granted by the National Association for Music Education (formerly Music Educators National Conference) since 1988, seven have been FSU students and students of Clifford's: Cornelia Yarbrough (1996), John Geringer (2000), Judith Jellison (2004), Robert Duke (2010), Patricia Flowers (2012), Wendy Sims (2016), and Harry Price (2018). Clifford was the inaugural recipient of the award.

One only need look at Clifford Madsen's scholarly output to admit that he is exceedingly productive and his students learn how to be consistently productive as well. One way that they learn this is by observing Clifford as he chooses how to spend his time. He modeled productivity, and it was inspiring because of his intense love of learning and research.

> His work ethic in this area is like no one else's. And, that for me and I'm sure for others, for you and for everybody else was probably the most incredible model you could ever have had. You know, rather than somebody telling you, you needed to do this, you just did it. As an ancillary part or as a primary part—and that model he provided was—what a great education!
>
> (Confredo, Deborah. Personal Interview. 16 March 2016)

Clifford taught productivity by first removing the fear of engaging in research, by reinforcing every attempt at research that he observed. Second, he avoided critiquing or providing forums for peer critiques of research, believing that this practice generated anxiety and impeded individuals' motivation to engage in research. Instead, he encouraged his students to present at every conference. Moreover, he expected it.

> You don't have a choice about being productive. You find a way to make it part of your life. And just the love of finding answers to questions. I would say those big global things now are what I think of instead of a particular topic.
>
> (Cassidy, Jane. Personal Interview. 3 June 2016)

"His productivity. Which doesn't stop. I mean he is still doing it. It is a great model" (Byo, James. Personal Interview. 2 June 2016). Clifford created a culture with graduate students where they were required to teach and research simultaneously, so that balancing between research and teaching became a natural expectation.

When one reviews Clifford's former students, one can see that many of them have become exceedingly productive. Because he encouraged his students to engage in research, numerous studies have been conducted that now contribute to the extant literature in music education and therapy.

> As you know, Cliff was a pioneer in the field of experimental research in music. Before him, there had been very little experimental activity in the profession. And when he started directing master's theses and doctoral dissertations, his graduate students were among the first students to do studies in that area, with their collective work adding significantly to the body of experimental literature.
>
> (Franklin, David. Personal Interview. 4 June 2016)

Michael Wagner elaborated on how Clifford encouraged productivity in his students by reinforcing their desire to learn and explore. "We [Cliff Madsen's students] continued throughout our career. We didn't do it to get promoted; we did it because it meant something. We did it because we were inquisitive, and we knew it mattered" (Wagner, Michael. Personal Interview. 5 June 2016).

Clifford prepared his students to be successful in their chosen profession, realizing that some students would go on to small universities and others would be at large, comprehensive universities and be asked to produce scholarship on a more frequent basis.

> I always enjoy teaching. But of course, Cliff set me straight when I was a doctoral student, that if I was going to survive at a large university—I mean, the carrot and the stick were there: "Get it done, get it done, get it done! What are you doing?" And that's where research conferences functioned and the music therapy association, because we had those every year, and I knew that he would support the research I was trying to do for poster research, but I still needed it to have integrity and to be something we could all be proud of. So, it was frankly the deadlines (*laughs*) that were incentives and the "You've got to do this."
>
> (Prickett, Carol. Personal Interview. 28 April 2016)

Astoundingly, Clifford never took a sabbatical in all of his years of teaching. He also did not believe that utilizing graduate students to assist with research was a tool for saving time and increasing his productivity: "Actually, students take a great deal of time if we do it correctly, as we always should, in order to help them to be truly independent scholars/teachers" (Personal Interview. 29 June 2015).[5] Further, his modeling of productivity with scholarship was a direct outcome of his love of research.

> Ultimately, if one wants to become a life-long scholar, one must develop a love for doing those things that scholars regularly do. Incentive systems such as merit, promotion and tenure function only for those who probably would be better served if they were to develop a "scholarly lifestyle" (Personal Interview. 29 June 2015).[6]

Personal Choice

Almost every one of Clifford's students referenced his lecture "Who Claps for You?" (see Chapter 6). The individual decides how to spend one's time, and chooses who is permitted to grant them approval and disapproval. So many people allow their environment or other people to control them. Habits, such as answering the phone immediately, opening the door when someone knocks, or responding immediately to the requests of others, were practices on which Clifford asked his students to reflect. Do you have to answer the phone when it rings? Or do you choose to answer the phone when it rings?

> You don't have to answer the phone, all the time. You have to know who is clapping for you and make decisions about whether you are going to jump when somebody snaps or not. Also, to recognize in yourself if you're treating other people like that.
>
> (Brittin, Ruth. Personal Interview. 17 March 2016)

> I learned that we don't have to answer the door just because someone is knocking, that we get to decide. We are not controlled by the phone ringing. We get to choose whether to answer the door or the phone on our own terms.
>
> (Sims, Wendy. Personal Interview. 17 March 2016)

Transfer

We asked Clifford's former students what lessons they hoped to share with their own students. Transfer was the concept most frequently mentioned. Everyone reflected on making transfers and thinking critically. Carl Hancock shared:

> If you think about something really, really deeply and you get into this mode where you start to make transfers, that can be very exciting for you mentally because you start to see that one idea refracts into a whole bunch of different others . . . you realize once again that there are only a few underlying concepts to everything and if you begin to understand that as a student or a teacher or a human being. Then you will start to see the connectivity and . . . you will just see there is more variety than there has ever been. And, I think that is one of the things, in terms of his legacy for me, is just in getting away from the notion of black and white and everything is gray but there is also an entire rainbow of colors connected to all that, too.
>
> (Hancock, Carl. Personal Interview. 17 March 2016)

Lindsey Williams recalled that he taught 28 different college courses over a nine-year period, and he attributed his success navigating the wide variety of courses to his ability to transfer, which was a skill he developed while under Clifford's tutelage.

> I would say the thread that connected all of that was both my being taught to think for transfer and my need to teach people to think for transfer, but I couldn't have taught all those different classes in as short a period of time as I did without having some sort of overarching umbrella.
>
> (Williams, Lindsey. Personal Interview. 16 March 2016)

Independence

After exploring the life and teaching of Clifford, it became abundantly clear that he wants his students and loved ones to be independent and happy. In order to be independent, individuals have to understand and choose their own values, pursue the things that make them happy within their value system, make choices, transfer knowledge, and thus become independent.

> The third lesson that I have really learned is that you have to create your own life and make sure that you create a life that you would love to live. You go into a job and if it's not the perfect job, make it the perfect job. When you are not the perfect parent, make yourself the perfect parent because you want to love your kids. Make your life with your spouse the type of life that you would want to have with a spouse. So, that taking responsibility for creating your own life's circumstances is really meaningful to me.
>
> (Cassidy, Jane. Personal Interview. 3 June 2016)

Interviews With the Madsen Children Concerning Their Parents

Clifford's children described very similar life lessons to those learned by his former students. Love, generosity, independence, kindness, empowering others, curiosity, and transfer were referenced frequently. Additionally, all of his children remembered poignant stories that highlighted the need to treat others with dignity and respect.

Sitka

From the time I was small, my parents provided a united front. I knew I could not pit one against the other to get what I wanted. If I tried to ask one parent for something, the one I thought would say yes, he/she would never say yes without saying, "Well, I have to discuss it with your mother/father and then I'll let you know." I never got to say, "Well, Mom/Dad said I could." I always had to wait until they discussed what I wanted. In this manner they always presented a united front for whatever decision was being made. On the other hand, I was given a lot of freedom. I remember on my sixteenth birthday, I wanted to go to Panama City Beach. I was allowed to borrow my mom's car for the weekend and go to the beach with some of my girlfriends. I think that showed a lot of trust in me on their part. I had been taught to be independent and responsible. For instance, I bought my own car, but my dad wouldn't begin teaching me how to drive until I learned how to change a tire. He also taught me to be self-reliant. When my car needed a repair, he told me to get three estimates for parts and labor and had me take it in for the repair.

My brother, sister, and I were taught to love one another and celebrate each other's successes. Whenever one of us got something the other didn't, we were taught to be happy for that person. I'm not sure, but I remember this starting with my dad taking one of us, at random, to the Dairy Queen for an ice cream. I am grateful to this day that I do not have issues with "fairness."

My father and mother taught me to be tolerant of others, of how important it was to not judge someone due to the color of their skin or religious beliefs. I remember someone in my fourth-grade class had a birthday party and invited everyone to the party—or so I thought. I felt awful when I discovered one girl who was black and one whose family was from India were not invited. I told my mom about this. She asked if I still wanted to go to the party. I said no. She asked if there was something I wanted to do instead. I remember thinking about it. I was allowed to ask both girls to go to the movies with me on the day of the party. This same year, God and religion came up in conversation at school. When the girl, whose family was from India, announced that there could be more than one God, other children verbally harassed her on a regular basis. I stood up for her, telling the others she could believe what she wanted. This was near the end of the school year and after this incident, most of my classmates didn't speak to me for the rest of the school year. Yet, because my parents also taught me to be a strong person and to do what was right, I was able to get through this time in my young life without once thinking that I should have kept quiet.

One of my father's priorities was focus of attention and concentration on the task at hand. We were never allowed to do homework with the television on. We sat at the kitchen table where it was quiet until we finished our homework. When practicing the piano, we practiced for a certain time period without distraction. When watching a movie, you learned not to talk and to focus on the movie. Now, no matter what is going on around me, I am able to focus on a task before me. I think this has also transferred to the belief that one should "live in the moment" regardless of whether it is for work or play.

My father was a heavy smoker for a number of years. But he quit "cold turkey." I don't know if it was because I wanted to try smoking one of his "dead" cigarettes or not. I do remember seeing one in a black plastic ash-tray and picking it up when I was very little. In any case, he didn't want his children smoking, so he quit. Years later, he told me one should model appropriate behavior, rather than just talk about it. He has always had a lot of will power and when he decides to do something, he does it.

My father taught us to have integrity. I still remember him talking about why somebody would ever steal paper from work, pens, or other things with disbelief. He would ask/exclaim, "Why would anyone want to sell their integrity over such little things—for a dollar or two?" I was taught to be honest by both my parents, to be honest and kind—to do my best at whatever I attempt to do and to have a passion for something.

Because of my father, I learned how to change an aspect of myself that I did not like using behavioral techniques. For example, I dreaded invitations to a party or a place where I would only know one person within a group of people. So, I drove my own car and told myself I could leave after I forced myself to go up to two people I didn't know at a social event and ask each person just one question. I then gradually increased the number of people and questions. The more I did it, the easier it got. Eventually, I even found myself having a good time. When I was in college, I took one of my father's teaching in higher education classes. It was one of the best experiences of my life. I still hated speaking in front of a group. His class was structured in a debate format, arguing the pros and cons of multiple issues in higher education. This helped me to get over my fear of public speaking and teaching a college class of my own. I remember he also provided feedback for every individual in that class, in a small handwritten note to be read in private. Mine was that I got too caught up in the subject matter. Since then, I have tried to remember to be aware of the person I am speaking to and not just the subject at hand.

Many of the things my father taught me were applicable to my job working with children. I value the most an appreciation for research. Based on research, he taught me the concept of error-free learning. It is better to have children learn something correctly the first time than to make them guess. Research has shown that variety in presentation, use of gestures, and other techniques also work well. I made sure to utilize these techniques during therapy, and to also help the teachers of my language-impaired students. Many teachers kept asking, "What is this?" I modeled how to teach the word/concept being taught. For example, if one were to teach a young child the names of zoo animals, a giraffe for instance, you would show the child a picture of a giraffe and say, "This is a giraffe!" Then you would show numerous pictures of giraffes, cartoon giraffes, drawings of giraffes, photos of giraffes as you modeled the name "giraffe" in various sentences such as, "This giraffe has spots. Ooh, look! This giraffe has spots too. The giraffes have long legs. And, the giraffes have long necks. That giraffe is eating leaves off the tree." You would also have stuffed giraffe toys and plastic giraffe animals to play with as you modeled the word giraffe. You would pretend to be a giraffe and stretch your neck to reach the leaves on a pretend tree. You would read a short book about a giraffe. At the end of a session, I loved giving my students a sticker/item we had made depicting a vocabulary word/concept. Then the teachers throughout the day would say, "I like your giraffe sticker," or "I like your giraffe magnet." And so forth. Hopefully, by the end of the session/day, the child has learned the target word taught, "giraffe," as well as other words such as "long," "tall," "spots," "leaves," and "silent," and where giraffes can be found, etc.

One of the most important things I know about my father is that he has insight to human behavior as a group and in specific individuals. He can analyze behavior very well and at the same time, he's compassionate and cares for the people that he teaches and/or helps. He doesn't just say, "Oh, you've got to change this behavior or that behavior." He listens and gives advice and truly wants to help people. And it is not just in their careers which he's concerned, it is in helping people be the best that they can be. I think he's able to do that because he has the charisma, because he has the insight, and is loved. I think if he didn't have that, he wouldn't be as successful as he is now.

(Lammert, Sitka. Personal Interview. 20 June 2016)

Cort

Both my parents were very much involved in the teaching process of their children. Both were teachers and behaviorists. When I was about seven or eight, integration was just taking place and my parents worked hard to teach us about the wrongfulness of racism and prejudice. In my third-grade year, busing began and Caroline Brevard Elementary became integrated. On the first day of school, all the whites sat on one side and the blacks on the other side of the classroom. The first thing the teacher did was assign seats based on alphabetical order. Within a few days, all the kids were playing just like kids do. Harold and Sylvester were two of my best friends, and my parents suggested that I invite them to the movies. This was a very thought-provoking experience that taught me about prejudice and privilege. First, I realized not everyone has a telephone. I had to call a neighbor of Sylvester's who went next door to go get him. Second, not that my family was well-to-do back then, but I noticed what real poverty looked like when my mother drove me to pick them up. Finally, I remember that we went to the Florida Theater, which in the early 1950s was segregated; the blacks sat in the balcony, while the whites were located at the bottom. I remember that just before the movie started, three high school kids walked past us to get to their seats. One of them told Harold, "Move your God damn nigger foot out of my way." I was mortified. I don't think that my parents ever envisioned that I would learn so much about life in that single afternoon, but looking back, at a minimum, they knew the teaching of potential friendship.

My parents always espoused the virtues of a diverse society, but sometimes one forgets the value of experiences and contexts. Living in West Windsor, which is a very affluent area of New Jersey just outside Princeton, one of my sons went over to a friend's house that was huge and much larger than his own. He came back from the playdate and asked in all seriousness, "Dad, are we poor?" My wife and I laughed telling our son that no, we were not poor. It reminded me of the time with Harold and Sylvester, and that my children had never experienced such an afternoon.

My sisters and I are very close. We were taught to always look out for each other. My dad would tell us the story of how he had to look out for his sister, Kaye, and hold her hand when they were going somewhere no matter what. It was the same when I walked my sister, Katia, down to her nursery school. My primary responsibility was to keep her safe.

My father expected us to meet our obligations. When I was a teenager my father cosigned a loan for me to buy a car. He told me that if I missed a single car payment, the car would be sold the next day. My father wanted me safe and prepared for any eventuality. He knew that sometimes the car would break down. He advised me to save a little bit each month to be prepared to repair the car when that happened. He told me that if I wore my seatbelt (this was in 1978, when seatbelts were not required or especially popular) in a consistent manner, he would give me \$100—and a hundred dollars was a lot of money at that time. The contingency was that I could never ask my dad about when I would earn the money, it just needed to be something that my dad noticed. It took a year, but when my dad realized it had become a habit, he gave me the \$100.

Both my parents strongly emphasized being self-reliant and having a strong work ethic. We were expected to have a job. Even when we were young, on Saturdays, my mom would write down a long list of all the chores that needed to be done. Each job paid a certain amount based on the difficulty of the task. Sitka and I would pick first, then alternate picking, initialing next to the jobs we wanted. Katia was the youngest child and had some of the easier chores that she could handle. We were also expected to do the dishes after our parents cooked, not for money, just for being a member of the household. My parents strongly believed that you are not entitled to anything in life. Nor did my father argue with his children. I laugh when I think of my father asking, "Do I answer 'why' questions?" It was his favorite line, making it very clear that the decisions of our parents were not up for discussion.

My father is the quintessential teacher. He loves to teach, and he knows how to teach. A lot of people like to show how smart they are, but that's not the "it," to use his own vernacular, for my father. His whole life has been dedicated to teaching and how to teach better. I also think that his students know deep down that he truly cares for them and has their best interests at heart. People are more likely to take advice and learn, knowing that. My father also taught by example. I remember after his car accident in 1968, when he went head first through the windshield and bits of pieces of glass were coming out of his head for the next five years, he was in a lot of pain. Dad used to sit on the couch for hours massaging his temple, but he never complained. Those were a couple of tough years for my family, and my mother did a great job of keeping everything together. Of course, you only appreciate the courage of them both when you are an adult and looking back. But, albeit a little late, the lesson is still there.

(Madsen, Cort. Personal Interview. 1 September 2016)

Katia

One of the things I admire most in my father is his courage and the example he has set for me. My dad would say that courage is doing the right thing not when it is easy, but when it is hard, when it is difficult, when it is unpopular. That in the face of adversity, one should be willing to act and not stay silent. And what is wonderful about my father, even in the face of his own strong sense of what is right or wrong, he can still discuss the intricacies of a subject and teach you to think for yourself. Discussing the human condition, my father has said there are times when you must stand up for people, and then understanding that there will be times when, in order to save a person's dignity, it is more important to stand with them. They don't need you to stand up for them, they need you to stand with them. The most courageous thing I think my father ever did was to leave the Mormon Church as a young man. This has nothing to do with the Mormon Church or any church. It has to do with one man's courage to live his personal truth. To not live a lie. To live authentically. Despite two loving parents and 11 brothers and sisters and countless relatives all adhering to Mormon doctrine, he was able to leave. He made that choice.

My father never sheltered me from the acquisition of knowledge. He made me aware of the civil rights issues at a very early age. I knew that people were putting their lives on the line and dying for the cause of civil rights. He has stood up for every minority group I can think of.

One of the things my father taught me was balance in life and forming relationships. He taught me conceptually about many things: empowerment without entitlement, loving without neediness, and provocative thinking without rumination. These are all ideas that he spun and discussed and challenged me to think about. He tells the story about "the green Life Saver," which I'm sure all his students have heard. A child offers you a sticky green Life Saver and you, of course, take it—a small lie, a good lie, to preserve someone's dignity and spirit.

It was important to my father that his children be empowered to make decisions for themselves and to be independent. For example, when I was about five years old, my parents took me to Disney World. When we departed the monorail, the first thing my father did was point to the Cinderella Castle and said, "If you get lost, you are going to walk to the Cinderella Castle. You are not going to cry. You are going to find a little family and walk behind them and act like you are with them. You get there and Mom and Dad will be there to get you. You just wait there as long as it takes. But, there you go. That's our plan." I mean, the first thing, of course, I look at my mom. "Am I going to get lost?" And she, "Clifford! No. . . ." But then my dad goes over it again. We are talking three or four minutes of my life in a moment. When he finished, I thought to myself, "Okay, if I get lost, I'm going to walk to that castle. I'm not going to cry. I'm going to act like I'm with that family and we're all fine. I will wait and my parents will find me." I believed it and I think what that did for me as a child was give me a sense of empowerment. "Yes, you can. Of course, you can." Not only that, "Hey, we have a plan. Right? If you get lost, we have a plan." And that is one of the things my dad teaches. To have a plan. To be prepared for any challenging situation or opportunity that may arise. "You are prepared. You've thought about it. Don't worry about it."

My father was a sweet-hearted man, and made my life a joy. When he wasn't teaching me, he was entertaining me.

(Madsen, Katia. Personal Interview. 15 April 2016)

Conclusions

Upon reflection on Clifford Madsen's philosophy and teaching and his students' memories, it is clear that he is a mentor who teaches students values, how to use time, how to make choices, encourages and facilitates transfer, and ultimately empowers people to be independent (see Figure 7.2).

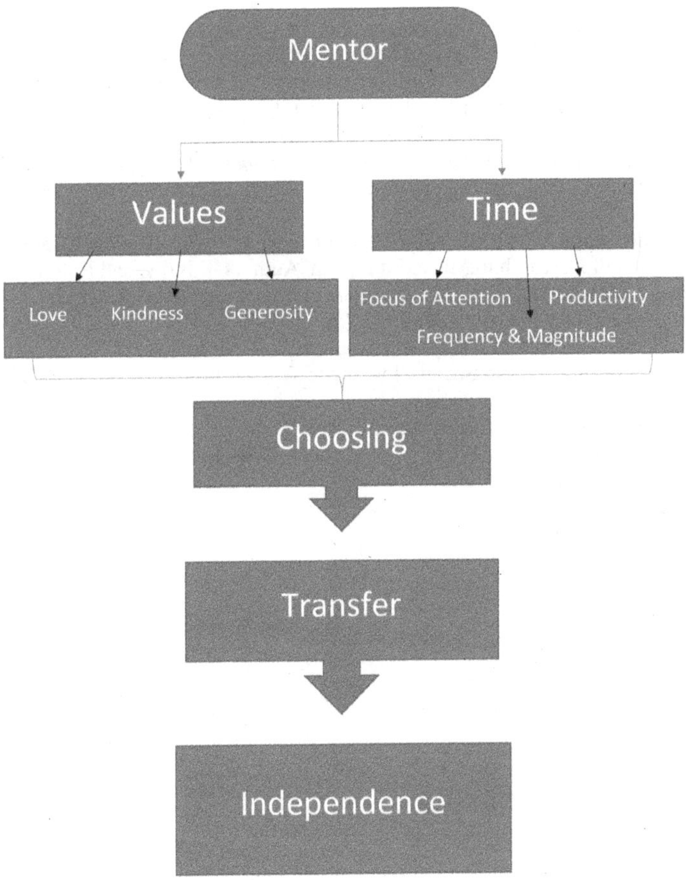

Figure 7.2 Clifford Madsen's educational model

Clifford's impact on the fields of music education and music therapy has been substantial. Many of his students have gone on to become important figures in their respective fields. The core principles of his philosophy, as viewed through the eyes of his students, can provide insight into how we can continue his legacy. The emergent themes in this study revealed that Clifford prioritized fostering a love of learning over delivering specific academic content. His ultimate goal was to empower individuals so that they were able to pursue their own personal goals.

Notes

1. Saldaña, Johnny. *The Coding Manual for Qualitative Researchers*. 2nd ed., SAGE Publications, Thousand Oaks, CA. 2016.
2. Campbell, John L., et al. "Coding In-Depth Semistructured Interviews: Problems of Unitization and Intercoder Reliability and Agreement." *Sociological Methods & Research*, vol. 42, no. 3, August 2013. Pp. 294–320.
3. Hodges, Don, et al. *Mastery Lessons from Eminent Music Education Scholars*. Paper presented at the Society for Music Teacher Education, Greensboro, NC. 2013.
4. Grashel, John. "Institutional Affiliation and Terminal Degree University of 'Journal of Research in Music Education' Authors, Editors, and Editorial Committee Members, 1990–2005." *Bulletin of the Council for Research in Music Education*, vol. 171, no. 171, 2007. Pp. 11.
5. Hodges, Don, et al. *Mastery Lessons from Eminent Music Education Scholars*. Paper presented at the Society for Music Teacher Education, Greensboro, NC. 2013.
6. Hodges, Don, et al. *Mastery Lessons from Eminent Music Education Scholars*. Paper presented at the Society for Music Teacher Education, Greensboro, NC. 2013.

Appendix

Complete List of Doctoral Students Advised

When Clifford Madsen first came to Florida State University (FSU), his interests were devoted to performing, teaching applied brass, teaching brass methods, and working with university bands. He did this for many years. As the years progressed, he began to gradually change his teaching emphasis to include courses in research methodology, music for the elementary teacher, the psychology of music, and behavior modification. However, from the beginning of his career at FSU, he continued to publish research. As he has been advising graduate students, and particularly doctoral students, this book has leaned heavily on those students who continued to do "research as their performing instrument," as Cornelia Yarbrough once declared. However, other students have taken different career paths while all making important contributions to music and music education. Some have become conductors, some have emphasized performance, some have become composers and/or arrangers, some administrators. Others have gone through different career transformations. Clifford never cared what career path students took. He just wanted them to be effective and happy in whatever they chose. Indeed, some of his closest loved ones are those doctoral students whose careers did not emphasize research. Additionally, even in research, he always emphasized that the research question was paramount, and the research question(s) should dictate the methodology used; and he advised doctoral students across all of these methodologies, including a plethora of individual topics.

Doctoral Students and Last Known Teaching Institution(s)

(This list includes doctoral students with co-major professors)

1. Dr. Frank Edmonson (1967): Head, Music Therapy Department, Napa Valley State Hospital (retired)
2. Dr. Alvin Wardle (1968): Utah State University (retired)
3. Dr. David Franklin (1968): Winthrop College (retired)
4. Dr. Fred Vorce (1969): Florida Department of Education (deceased)

5. Dr. Peter Temko (1971): University of Tennessee at Chattanooga (retired)
6. Dr. Julian White (1972): Florida Agricultural and Mechanical University (retired)
7. Dr. Jere L. Forsythe (1971): Ohio State University (retired)
8. Dr. Terry L. Kuhn (1972): Kent State University (retired)
9. Dr. Judith Jellison (1972): University of Texas, Austin (retired)
10. Dr. Cornelia Yarbrough (1973): Louisiana State University (retired)
11. Dr. Michael J. Wagner (1973): Florida International University (retired)
12. Dr. Kenneth Murray (1973): Wingate College (retired)
13. Dr. Bert Dameron (1973): Ohio University (retired)
14. Dr. Randall S. Moore (1974): University of Oregon (retired)
15. Dr. Charles P. Alley (1976): Freelance Musician
16. Dr. John M. Geringer (1976): University of Texas, Austin; Florida State University
17. Dr. Dawn C. Wooderson (1977): Pennsylvania State University; Southern Methodist University; Baylor University (retired)
18. Dr. Rita Salzberg (1977): University of Kentucky; Director, Music Program, Alabama School of the Arts (retired)
19. Dr. Juanita McElwain (1978): University of New Mexico; Phillips University (retired)
20. Dr. David E. Wolfe (1979): University of the Pacific (retired)
21. Dr. Robert Spradling (1980): Syracuse University; Western Michigan University (retired)
22. Dr. Patricia J. Flowers (1981): University of Texas, San Antonio; Ohio State University; Dean, Florida State University
23. Dr. Myra J. Staum (1981): Willamette University; State University of New York, New Paltz (retired)
24. Dr. Robert A. Duke (1983): Kent State University; University of Texas, Austin
25. Dr. Alice-Ann Darrow (1983): University of Kansas; Florida State University
26. Dr. Carol A. Prickett (1983): University of Alabama (retired)
27. Dr. Charles E. Furman (1984): University of Minnesota (deceased)
28. Dr. Vincent Kantorski (1984): Bowling Green University
29. Dr. Wendy Sims (1985): University of Missouri, Columbia
30. Dr. Larry Blocher (1986): Wichita State University; Dean, Troy University Alabama
31. Dr. David S. Smith (1987): University of Georgia; Western Michigan University
32. Dr. Brian Knudson (1987): Dickinson State University
33. Dr. Jane Cassidy (1988): Louisiana State University

34. Dr. Jim Byo (1988): Louisiana State University
35. Dr. Earlene Rentz (1988): Baylor University; Freelance Composer
36. Dr. Charles Robinson (1988): University of Missouri, Kansas City
37. Dr. Ruth Brittin (1989): Syracuse University; University of the Pacific
38. Dr. Deborah Sheldon (1991): Illinois State University; University of Illinois; Temple University (retired)
39. Dr. Peggy Codding (1992): Ohio University; Berklee College of Music
40. Dr. Christopher Johnson (1992): University of Kansas
41. Dr. William Fredrickson (1992): University of Missouri, Kansas City; Florida State University
42. Dr. Janna Brendell (1992): East Carolina University (retired)
43. Dr. James Tipps (1992): Wayne State University
44. Dr. Roy Legette (1993): Shorter College; University of Georgia
45. Dr. Bobby Adams (1994): Stetson University (deceased)
46. Dr. Michael Bell (1994): Case Western Reserve University
47. Dr. Michael Heaney (1994): Director of Music, Haverford School, Philadelphia; The Southport School, Southport, Australia
48. Dr. Suzanne Byrnes (1994): Director, Kansas City Children's Choir; Children's Choir, Florida State University
49. Dr. John Lychner (1995): Western Michigan University; Stetson University
50. Dr. David Frego (1996): Ohio State University; University of Texas, San Antonio; Penn State University
51. Dr. Dale Meisenhelter (1996): University of Arkansas, Fayetteville
52. Dr. John Coggiola (1997): Syracuse University
53. Dr. Steven White (1997): Eastern Kentucky University
54. Dr. Kenneth Williams (1998): University of Texas, San Antonio; Jacksonville County Schools
55. Dr. Keith Kaiser (1998): Ithaca College
56. Dr. Wayne Goins (1998): Kansas State University
57. Dr. J. Jossim (1999): Florida Southern University
58. Dr. Ann Porter (2000): California State University, Hayward [now known as California State University, East Bay]; Cincinnati Conservatory
59. Dr. Elisa Macedo-Dekaney (2001): Syracuse University
60. Dr. Rick Fleming (2001): State University of New York, Buffalo
61. Dr. Carolyn Fulton (2001): Florida International University; International School, Bangkok, Thailand (retired)
62. Dr. Kerstin Herkstroeter (2001): Los Angeles County Schools
63. Dr. Rick Crowley (2001): South Dakota State University
64. Dr. Carl Hancock (2002): University of Arizona; University of Alabama, Tuscaloosa
65. Dr. Joe Parisi (2002): University of Missouri, Kansas City

66. Dr. John Falskow (2002): Landers University; Bremerton Symphony, Tacoma, Washington
67. Dr. John Southall (2003): University of Missouri, St. Louis; Indian River Community State College; Florida State University
68. Dr. Phyllis Paul (2003): University of Oregon; Youngstown State University
69. Dr. Lindsey Williams (2004): Kansas State University, Manhattan; University of Missouri, Kansas City; West Virginia University; Fine Arts Director, Seminole County Public Schools
70. Dr. Debbie Chandler (2004): University of Louisiana at Monroe
71. Dr. David Plack (2006): Florida State University
72. Dr. Jessica Nápoles (2006): University of Utah; University of North Texas
73. Dr. Grieg Woodward (2006): Truett McConnell University
74. Dr. Paul Dease (2007): Magic City Choral Society, Birmingham, Alabama; Midwestern State University
75. Dr. Amy Acklin (2008): University of Louisville
76. Dr. Jay Juchniewicz (2008): East Carolina University
77. Dr. Eric Simpson (2009): Texas Christian University
78. Dr. Frank Diaz (2010): University of Oregon; Indiana University, Bloomington
79. Dr. Carol Payne (2010): Clayton State University
80. Dr. Jonathan Hinkle (2011): University of Colorado, Mesa
81. Dr. Jay Silveira (2011): Oregon State University, Ithaca; University of Oregon
82. Dr. Jeffery Redding (2012): West Virginia University; Orlando Public Schools
83. Dr. Michael Hudson (2012): University of Kentucky
84. Dr. Edward Kawakami (2014): Carthage College. Kenosha, Wisconsin.
85. Dr. Chandler Bridges (2016): Northern Alabama University; Indiana University
86. Dr. Rachel Friedman (2017): Freelance Conductor
87. Dr. Annalisa Chang (2017): Clayton State University
88. Dr. Thomas Singletary (2017): Moorhead State University; Texas Christian University
89. Dr. Clara Knotts (2017): Leon County Schools, Tallahassee, Florida
90. Dr. Robert Clark (2018): Georgia Southeastern University; Vanderbilt University
91. Dr. Julia Baumanis (2019): University of Central Missouri
92. Dr. Aisha Ivey (2019): Florida State University

Index

Note: Page numbers in *italic* indicate a photo and page numbers in **bold** indicate a figure.